Intermediate Commercial Correspondence

Intermediate Commercial Correspondence wurde geplant und entwickelt von der Redaktion Moderne Fremdsprachen des Cornelsen Verlags, Berlin.

Verfasser:	David Clarke, Witten
	Dieter Wessels, Bochum
Kritische Durchsicht:	Bob Muscutt, Solingen
Projektleitung:	Jim Austin
Verlagsredaktion:	Andreas Goebel
Redaktionelle Mitarbeit:	Kari-ann Seamark
Layout und technische Umsetzung:	Petra Eberhard, Berlin
Illustration:	Oxford Designers & Illustrators
Titelbild:	Getty Images

> Erhältlich sind auch:
> **Audio-CD** (ISBN 978-3-464-02809-4)
> **Answer key** (ISBN 978-3-464-02801-8)
> **Elementary Commercial Correspondence** (ISBN 978-3-464-01992-4)
> **Advanced Commercial Correspondence** (ISBN 978-3-464-02790-5)

www.cornelsen.de

Die Links zu externen Webseiten Dritter, die in diesem Lehrwerk angegeben sind, wurden vor Drucklegung sorgfältig auf ihre Aktualität geprüft. Der Verlag übernimmt keine Gewähr für die Aktualität und den Inhalt dieser Seiten oder solcher, die mit ihnen verlinkt sind.

1. Auflage, 5. Druck 2014

Alle Drucke dieser Auflage sind inhaltlich unverändert und können im Unterricht nebeneinander verwendet werden.

© 2004 Cornelsen Verlag, Berlin
© 2014 Cornelsen Schulverlage GmbH, Berlin

Das Werk und seine Teile sind urheberrechtlich geschützt. Jede Nutzung in anderen als den gesetzlich zugelassenen Fällen bedarf der vorherigen schriftlichen Einwilligung des Verlages. Hinweis zu den §§ 46, 52a UrhG: Weder das Werk noch seine Teile dürfen ohne eine solche Einwilligung eingescannt und in ein Netzwerk eingestellt oder sonst öffentlich zugänglich gemacht werden.
Dies gilt auch für Intranets von Schulen und sonstigen Bildungseinrichtungen.

Druck: Offizin Andersen Nexö Leipzig

ISBN 978-3-464-02800-1

 Inhalt gedruckt auf säurefreiem Papier aus nachhaltiger Forstwirtschaft.

Inhalt

1	Form and layout of business letters	4
2	Office communication: telephoning	14
3	Office communication: emails	25
4	Enquiries	37
5	Offers and quotations	48
6	Orders and acknowledgements	58
7	Dealing with orders	69
8	Payments and reminders	82
9	Complaints	94
10	Applying for a job	106
	Musterprüfungen	118
	Deutsch–englisches Glossar	127
	Alphabetisches Wörterverzeichnis	132
	Transcripts	138
	Incoterms	143
	Packing containers and materials	144

1 Form and layout of business letters

What is a business letter?

- Business letters – and facsimile messages ('faxes') and emails – are written by one firm, organisation or individual to another about business matters *(Geschäftsangelegenheit)*. The writer of the letter etc is the **sender**; the receiver is the **addressee**.

- A **fax** is a business letter that is sent electronically, usually down a phone line. Although the layout may be different, the style of faxes is the same as that of business letters.

- An **email** is more like a spoken message in written form. For this reason, emails tend to make use of short forms *(didn't, he's, they've)* and a more conversational style, for example, *This is to let you know that the goods arrived here safely today*, instead of the more formal, *This is to confirm that the goods were safely delivered to our premises today*.

- The **aim** of routine business letters and faxes is to …
  … give the addressee information: *The goods left our stores on 15 May.*
  … ask the addressee for information: *When did the goods leave your stores?*
  … ask the addressee to do something: *Please confirm receipt of this order.*

- When you write to a firm for the first time, say **who** you are, **where** you got the firm's address from and **what** you want the addressee to do. If you are writing to a firm you already know, just say **why** you are writing and **what** you want.

> Always obey the **ABC Rule** when you write a business letter, fax or email:
>
> **A** Be **accurate**. Make sure that all details, i.e. names, dates, references, order numbers, prices etc, are correct and complete.
>
> **B** Be **brief**. Say what you want to say and then stop. Always keep strictly to the point *(beim Thema bleiben)*.
>
> **C** Be **clear**. Use plain, simple English. Never use unnecessarily technical language or 'jargon'. Write in an easy, natural style without being either too formal or too familiar. However, use **long forms**, e.g. *they are, he did not, they would be*, in business correspondence.

Model letter

Ahrens & Kessler GmbH in Bremen is a wholesale supplier of outdoor clothing and footwear. In this enquiry, Karin Feldmann in Purchasing asks Robert Carr & Co Ltd, a British manufacturer of wax coats and jackets, to send her their latest catalogue.

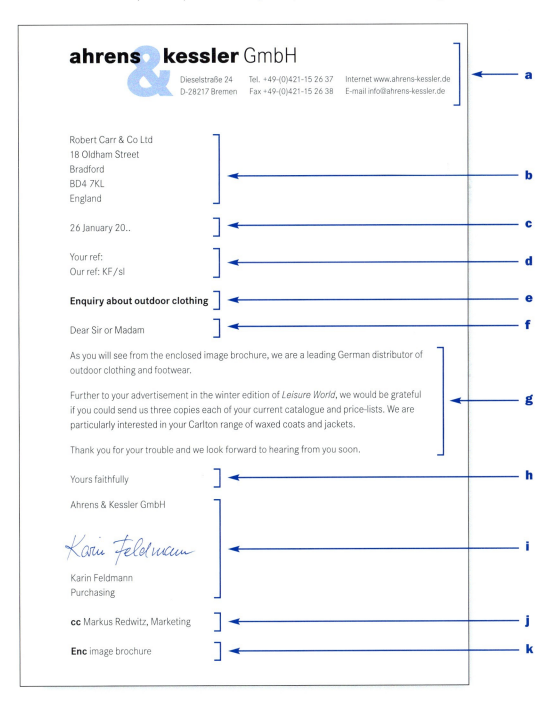

a Are these statements true, false or you can't say because of lack of information? Correct the false statements.

1 The letter is addressed to Ahrens & Kessler in Bremen.
2 The letter was signed by Karin Feldmann.
3 Karin is Ahrens & Kessler's purchasing manager.
4 The image brochure is in four colours.
5 Ahrens & Kessler is particularly interested in footwear.
6 Robert Carr & Co advertised in *Leisure World*.

b Look at parts a–k of the letter again. Match them with the terms 1–11 below.

1 complimentary close
2 copy circulated / carbon copy
3 date
4 enclosures
5 inside address
6 letterhead
7 body of letter
8 reference
9 salutation
10 signature block
11 subject line

c Turn the letter below into a more informal email by replacing the underlined words and expressions with items from the box.

> advert | attached PDF document | Best wishes | Good morning
> let us have | seller | Thanks a lot | we'd be glad | We're especially keen on
> we're | you'll | latest

Dear Sir or Madam [1]

As you will [2] see from the enclosed image brochure [3], we are [4] a leading German distributor [5] of outdoor clothing and footwear.

Further to your advertisement [6] in the winter edition of Leisure World, we would be grateful [7] if you could send us [8] three copies each of your current [9] catalogue and price-lists. We are particularly interested in [10] your Carlton range of waxed coats and jackets.

Thank you [11] for your trouble and we look forward to hearing from you soon.

Yours faithfully [12]

Karin Feldmann

B Notes on business letters

1 Format and layout

There is no standard format or layout for business letters in English, so you can use the German DIN-form if you prefer.

However, in modern business correspondence, the **American block form** has become almost standard practice throughout the English-speaking world. Here the parts are simply listed one after the other on the left. In this book, we have used the American block form throughout.

> Note that in the block form, **no commas** are used in addresses (b), at the end of the subject line (e), and after the salutation and complimentary close (f, h). This is called 'open punctuation'. In the body of the letter, normal punctuation is used.

2 Letterhead (a)   *Briefkopf*

As there are no fixed 'rules' about company letterheads in the English-speaking world, they vary widely from one company to another. However, they always show **a)** the company's registered name and address, and perhaps its registration number, **b)** its telephone and fax numbers and **c)** almost always its e-mail and/or website addresses. Note that when answering a letter, the inside address (see below) of your letter must always be exactly the same as the letterhead of the original letter.

3 Inside address (b)   *Empfängeranschrift*

The inside address shows who the letter is to, i.e. the name and address of the addressee. If you are not using a window envelope, make sure that the address on the envelope is exactly the same as the inside address. If you are replying to a letter, always copy the inside address from the letterhead of the original letter (see **2** above).

Look at these examples of British and American addresses.

UK
Outside London

Anglian Freight Co Ltd	no point after **Co** (Company) and **Ltd** (Limited)
12 Essex Road	building number before street name
Ipswich	postal town alone
IP4 9HJ	postcode alone
United Kingdom	name of country, i.e. United Kingdom

London addresses

London Insurance Co Ltd	no point after **Co** (Company) and **Ltd** (Limited)
38 Vienna Gardens	building number before street name
London SW1 7GH	London + space + postcode; no country with London addresses

USA

Western Electronics Inc.	point after Inc. (Incorporated)
182 Edison Avenue	building number before street name
Dallas, TX 76432	comma + space between postal town and ZIP code
U.S.A.	U.S.A. 'closed', i.e. with points

> **Always** use the official two-letter abbreviations for US states – e.g. **TX** for **Texas** – in ZIP-codes. This is important because the US Postal Service does not guarantee delivery of mail with incorrect codes.
>
> **ZIP code abbreviations of names of US states**
>
> | | | | | | |
> |---|---|---|---|---|---|
> | Alabama | AL | Kentucky | KY | North Dakota | ND |
> | Alaska | AK | Louisiana | LA | Ohio | OH |
> | Arizona | AZ | Maine | ME | Oklahoma | OK |
> | Arkansas | AR | Maryland | MD | Oregon | OR |
> | California | CA | Massachusetts | MA | Pennsylvania | PA |
> | Colorado | CO | Michigan | MI | Rhode Island | RI |
> | Connecticut | CT | Minnesota | MN | South Carolina | SC |
> | Delaware | DE | Mississippi | MS | South Dakota | SD |
> | District of Columbia | DC | Missouri | MO | Tennessee | TN |
> | Florida | FL | Montana | MT | Texas | TX |
> | Georgia | GA | Nebraska | NE | Utah | UT |
> | Hawaii | HI | Nevada | NV | Vermont | VT |
> | Idaho | ID | New Hampshire | NH | Virginia | VA |
> | Illinois | IL | New Jersey | NJ | Washington | WA |
> | Indiana | IN | New Mexico | NM | West Virginia | WV |
> | Iowa | IA | New York | NY | Wisconsin | WI |
> | Kansas | KS | North Carolina | NC | Wyoming | WY |

> **Universal Postal Union**
>
> The **Universal Postal Union** is a division of the United Nations. Go to its website at www.upu.int to find out how to write addresses in over 180 countries.
>
> On the UPU's **homepage**, click **Addressing** in the **Resources** menu, and then **Postal Addressing Systems in Member Countries** in the **Addressing** menu. Then scroll to the country you want and click **Display**.

4 Date (c)   *Datum*

There is no standard way of writing the date in English. In **general usage**, all the following forms are acceptable, though forms with the **day after the month** are more common in the USA:

12th April 2005	ordinal number – month – year
12 April 2005	cardinal number – month – year
April 12th, 2005	month – ordinal number + comma – year
April 12, 2005	month – cardinal number + comma – year

However, **12 April 2005** is by far the most common form in modern business usage.

> Be careful with 'all-number dates' like **11.6.04, 11/6/04** and **11-6-04**. In Europe these mean **11 June 2004**, but in North America and some Asian countries, including Japan, they mean **6 November 2004**.
>
> For this reason, it is best to avoid all-number dates in external business letters and documents, although you can use them in internal notes and memos, and in private correspondence.

5 **Reference** (d)   *Bezugszeichen*

When answering a business letter, always give the reference of the original letter under **Your ref:** *(Ihr Zeichen)* and your own reference under **Our ref:** *(Unser Zeichen)*.

References normally show **a)** who wrote the letter and **b)** who typed it. However, they may also give other details, such as the date or an identity number. The writer's initials come first, usually in capitals, followed by the typist's initials in small letters, for example **KF/sl** (see model letter).

6 **Salutation** (e)   *Anrede*

If you know the name of the person who will deal with your letter, then use it, for example, **Dear Ms Carter** or **Dear Mr Hammond**. If you normally use the other person's first name, then use it in business communications as well, for example, **Dear Helen** or **Dear Jim**.

Note that the neutral form **Ms** [mɪz:] is the standard form of address for women in business situations. This is because the traditional forms **Miss** (for unmarried women) and **Mrs** (for married, divorced or widowed women) depend on a woman's marital status, i.e. on her relationship to a man. This dependence is thought inappropriate in modern usage. If you don't know the person's name, use the impersonal form **Dear Sir or Madam**. In some American and Canadian letters, you may see **Ladies and Gentlemen:**, or even **Gentlemen:**, but in normal business usage this salutation is now going out of use.

Note that in the American and Canadian form **Mr., Mrs., Ms.** and the academic title **Dr.** are written with a point, but in the British form they are 'open' (**Mr, Mrs, Ms, Dr**).

7 **Subject line** (f)   *Betreffzeile*

The subject line says what the letter is about in as few words as possible. It is usually written **in bold** or underlined, for example, **Enquiry about outdoor clothes** or Enquiry about outdoor clothes. In the American form, the subject line may start with the word **Subject:**, but this is unusual in British usage.

Note that the **subject line** can come before or after the salutation according to company practice. However, if in doubt, position it **before** the salutation as in the model letter on page 5.

8 **Body of letter** (g)   *Brieftext*

The text of a business letter is called 'body'.

To help the reader, when you write the body of a business letter, always use one paragraph for each point and leave a space ('white line') between each paragraph.

9 **Complimentary close** (h)   *Grußformel*

Always finish your letter with a complimentary close. You can choose the most appropriate formulation from the table on the following page.

UK and Commonwealth except Canada

	Salutation	Complimentary close	Formality
Impersonal	Dear Sir or Madam	Yours faithfully	formal
Personal	Dear Lisa	Yours	friendly
		Yours sincerely	quite formal
	Dear Mr Cobb	Yours sincerely	neutral

USA and Canada

	Salutation	Complimentary close	Formality
Impersonal	Dear Sir or Madam	Yours truly	formal
	Ladies and Gentlemen:	Truly yours	
		Very truly yours	
Personal	Dear Nick,	Yours	friendly
		Sincerely yours	neutral
		Yours sincerely	quite formal
	Dear Ms. Harper	Sincerely yours	neutral
		Yours sincerely	

> If you know the other person very well, you can use **With best/kind regards** (*Viele Grüße*) or **With best wishes** (*Mit den besten Wünschen*).

10 Signature block (i)   *Unterschriften*

In the **signature block**, the name of the company often comes above the writer's signature, and his or her position within the company below it.

If the letter is signed by somebody other than the writer, then this must be made clear by putting **for** or, more formally, **on behalf of** immediately before the writer's name below the signature, for example:

Yours faithfully
Robert Carr & Company Limited

Peter Edwards

For / On behalf of Helen Shaw
Sales Manager

11 Copies (j)   *Verteiler*

The letters **cc** originally stood for **carbon copy/copies**. However, 'cc' also stands for **copy/copies circulated**, which has been suggested as a sensible modern alternative. After all, nowadays there are no 'carbon copies' (*Durchschläge*).

If the sender does not want the addressee to know that other people have been sent copies of the letter, then **bcc** for **blind copy/copies circulated** is put onto the **file copy** of the letter (for example: bcc Jonathan Barker, Legal Department).

12 Enclosures (k)   *Anlagen*

If you put something into the envelope with the letter, then say so under **Enc** (or **Encl**) for one item or **Encs** (or **Encls**) for two or more items.

C Practising language

1 Write out these abbreviations in full.

1 bcc   *blind copy circulated*
2 cc   ...
3 Co   ...
4 email ...
5 enc   ...
6 encls ...
7 fax   ...
8 Ltd   ...
9 tel   ...

2 There are two mistakes in each of these addresses. Find the mistakes and correct them.

a Aubade Automotive Parts Ltd
   Rose Lane 47
   Norwich, NR1 7UH
   England

b United Oil Inc.
   267, Delaware Road
   TX 67432, Dallas
   U.S.A.

c Thomas Low Ltd.
   45 Surrey Docks
   London
   E1 8HJ

d Union Bank of Scotland PLC
   12 Balmoral Square,
   Inverness
   Scotland
   IN2 8DS

e Ms. Laurie Bond,
   438 Ocean Boulevard
   Los Angeles
   CA 62371
   U.S.A.

3 Write out these dates and then read them out to your partner. Look at the example first.

EXAMPLE: 19.11.02   write: *19 November 2002*
                      say: the nineteenth of November, two thousand (and) two

1 25.4.92   ...
2 7.12.00   ...
3 15.2.02   ...
4 5.3.03   ...
5 10.08.38 ...
6 31.01.01 ...

4 You have received a record of deliveries with all-number dates from a Japanese supplier. Write out the dates in a European form. Don't forget that in these dates, the month comes before the day.

1 11/03/00   *3 November 2000*
2 01/05/01   ...
3 08/09/02   ...
4 05/08/03   ...

5 Use numbers 1–4 to link the salutations to a suitable complimentary close, a–d. In one case, more than one solution is possible.

1	Dear Sir or Madam	a	Yours
2	Dear Martin	b	Yours sincerely
3	Ladies and Gentlemen	c	Yours faithfully
4	Dear Ms Adams	d	Very truly yours

6 This letter from Robert Carr & Co Ltd to Ahrens & Kessler GmbH is complete, but the parts are in the wrong order. Write out the complete letter in the correct order.

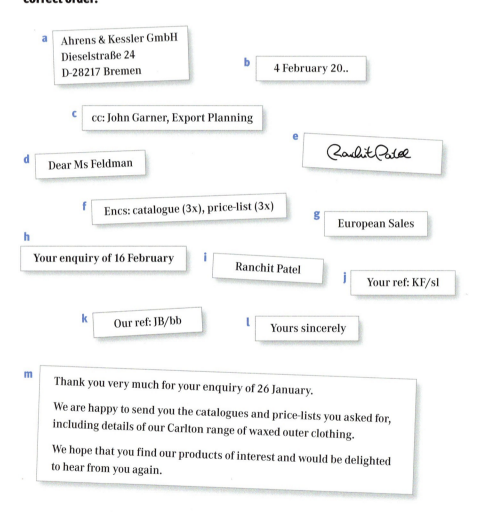

D Unit word list

Page 4	sender	*Absender/in*
	addressee	*Adressat/in, Empfänger/in*
Page 5	wholesale	*Großhandel*
	supplier	*Lieferant*
	purchasing	*Beschaffung, Einkauf*
	manufacturer	*Hersteller/in*
	catalogue	*Katalog*
	enquiry	*Anfrage*
	enclosed	*anbei, beiliegend*
	brochure	*Prospekt, Broschüre*
	distributor	*Vertrieb(sgesellschaft)*
	advertisement	*Anzeige*
	grateful	*dankbar*
	edition	*Ausgabe*
	price-list	*Preisliste*
	particularly	*besonders, insbesondere*
	to be interested in	*sich interessieren für*
	range	*Sortiment, Produktpalette*
	to look forward to	*sich freuen auf*
	cc / carbon copy, copy circulated	*Durchschlag, Kopie*
	Enc / enclosure	*Anlage*
Page 6	to address	*adressieren*
	to sign	*unterschreiben*
	to advertise	*Werbung machen*
	reference	*Bezugszeichen*
	subject line	*Betreffzeile*
Page 7	registered name	*eingetragener Firmenname*
	registration number	*Registernummer, hier: Steuernummer*
	window envelope	*Fensterumschlag*
	copy	*abschreiben*
	post code, ZIP code	*Postleitzahl*
	space	*Leerstelle*
Page 8	abbreviation	*Abkürzung*
	to guarantee	*garantieren*
Page 9	type	*tippen*
	initials	*Initialen*
Page 10	for / on behalf of	*im Auftrag von*
Page 12	record	*Liste, Übersicht*
	delivery	*Lieferung*
	details	*Einzelheiten*
Useful words	to forward	*nachsenden*
	under separate cover	*mit getrennter Post*
	by air mail	*mit Luftpost*
	registered mail	*Einschreiben*
	by express, special delivery	*durch Eilboten*
	return if undelivered	*Zurück, falls unzustellbar*

Office communication: telephoning

Model phone calls: asking to speak to somebody; arranging appointments

Useful phrases: asking to speak to somebody (phoning somebody, answering the phone, putting a caller through, saying somebody is not available, offering help, asking for information, getting out of trouble, saying goodbye); arranging appointments (asking for an appointment, fixing a time and date, accepting and rejecting suggestions, closing)

Telephoning in business

In spite of the huge increase in electronic mailing in the form of emails, text messaging and faxes, it is hard to exaggerate the importance of telephoning in business.

Telephoning is the main means of communication in countless situations, both as **internal calls** within the same company and as **external calls** with customers and suppliers. In an increasingly global economy, a large number of external calls are carried out in English, which is now the common language (*lingua franca*) of international business.

Routine telephone calls

This section introduces you to the language you need to make routine telephone calls in these basic business situations:

1 Calling a person in his or her office.
2 Leaving a message.
3 Making appointments and arranging visits.

The situation

Sam Kavanagh is an Irish manufacturer of quality outdoor clothing. Sam wants to market his Stormy Weather range of products in Germany, so he asks the German Embassy in Dublin for advice. The embassy gives Sam the names of some specialist German marketing organisations that help companies to sell their products in Germany.

Sam's first choice is UB Consult GmbH, a fashion consultancy in Düsseldorf. Sam chooses this firm because UB Consult is very experienced, and has good contacts to the Netherlands and Scandinavia as well. He also likes the idea of dealing directly with the joint owners, Uwe Bach and his wife Ulla.

A Taking notes

1 Making and answering calls

In this dialogue, Sam Kavanagh is calling Ulla Bach of UB Consult for the first time. Unfortunately, Ulla is not in her office so the person taking the call, Ulla's secretary, Lisa Schmitz, asks if she can take a message.

a You are Lisa. Listen to the dialogue and note down the following information.

1. Who is calling?
2. What does the caller want?
3. What does the caller want Lisa to do?
4. What is the caller's phone number?
5. Why is the message 'quite urgent'?

b Note down the English equivalents of the German expressions and sentences. Work with a partner. One of you concentrates on the even numbers, the other on the odd.

1. Haben Sie etwas dagegen, wenn ich …
2. Überhaupt nicht. Nur zu.
3. Wer spricht, bitte?
4. Könnten Sie bitte das für mich buchstabieren?
5. Bleiben Sie bitte dran.
6. Ich verbinde Sie weiter.
7. (Ms Bach) ist nicht in ihrem Büro.
8. Kann ich ihr etwas ausrichten?
9. Das habe ich notiert.
10. Bitte schön.

c Listen again and note down who or what the pronouns in *italics* refer to. Look at the example first.

EXAMPLE   Do *you* mind if *I* speak English?
           '*You*' is Lisa, and '*I*' is Sam.

1. Could *you* spell that for *me*, please?
2. Yes, *that's* right, but *we* don't pronounce *them*.
3. *She* had to go out, *I'm* afraid.
4. Can *you* ask her to ring *me*, please?
5. Could *you* tell *her* *it's* quite urgent?
6. *I'll* make sure *she* has *your* message as soon as *she* gets back.

UNIT 2 Office communication: telephoning

2 Arranging appointments

In this dialogue, Sam Kavanagh's secretary, Kate Connors, is calling Lisa Schmitz to arrange an appointment for her boss to meet the Bachs at the ispo Sportmode fair in Munich, which they are all attending. Note the use of first names, which is usual in the English-speaking world.

a **Listen to the phone conversation and complete Lisa's email to Kate with the missing details.**

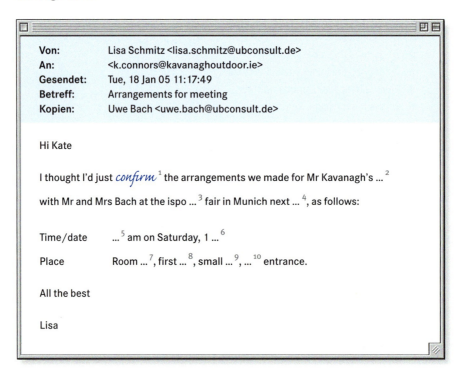

b **Put in the missing prepositions. Then check your answers by listening to the phone conversation again. Not all the answers are in the conversation.**

1. What can I do ... you?
2. Sam and the Bachs are meeting ...[1] a fair ...[2] Munich ...[3] February.
3. They want to meet ...[1] the first day ...[2] the fair.
4. Uwe Bach has booked a room ...[1] the small conference centre ...[2] Saturday morning.
5. The conference centre is ...[1] the Theresienhöhe entrance ...[2] the exhibition ground.
6. The room ...[1] which the meeting is taking place is ...[2] the first floor ...[3] the conference centre.

B Telephoning language

1 Making and answering calls

Phoning somebody

Mein Name ist ... Kann ich bitte mit Herrn / Frau ... sprechen?	My name's ... Can/Could/May I speak to Mr/Ms ..., please?
Könnte ich bitte jemanden vom Einkauf / Verkauf / von der Buchhaltung sprechen?	Can/Could/May I speak to somebody in purchasing/sales/accounts/..., please?
Kann ich bitte jemanden sprechen, der für Marketing / für den Verkauf zuständig ist?	Can/Could/May I speak to whoever is in charge of / responsible for marketing/sales/ ..., please?

Good morning	*Guten Morgen*	00:00 to 12:00
Good afternoon	*Guten Tag*	12:00 to 18:00
Good evening	*Guten Abend*	18:00 to 24:00

Note that in ordinary English **good day** is is no longer used as a greeting.

Answering the phone

Guten Morgen/Tag. (Firma). Kann ich Ihnen helfen?	Good morning/afternoon. ... Can I help you / How can I help you?
Mit wem spreche ich bitte / Wie ist bitte Ihr Name?	Who's calling / May I have your name, please?

Putting a caller through

Bleiben Sie bitte kurz dran? Ich stelle Sie zum Export / zu ... durch.	Can/Could you hold the line, please? I'll put you through to export / to ...
Einen Augenblick bitte. Ich schau mal, ob ich ... erreichen kann.	Just one moment, please. I'll see if ... is available/free.

Saying somebody is not available

Tut mir Leid, aber ... ist momentan nicht erreichbar.	I'm sorry, but ... is not available/free at the moment.
... ist leider gerade nicht am Platz / in seinem/ ihrem Büro.	I'm afraid ... is not at his/her desk / not in his/her office at present.
Tut mir Leid, aber ... ist nicht da / heute nicht im Büro.	I'm sorry, but ... is away / out of the office today.
Tut mir Leid, aber ... ist gerade in einer Besprechung.	I'm sorry, but ... is in a meeting at the moment.
... ist leider (gerade) zu Tisch / im Urlaub.	I'm afraid that ... is at lunch / on holiday.
Tut mir Leid, aber ... spricht gerade auf einer anderen Leitung.	I'm sorry, but ... is speaking on another line at present.

Offering help

Kann ich ... etwas ausrichten?	Can I take a message for ...?
Möchten Sie später noch einmal anrufen, oder soll ... Sie zurückrufen?	Would you like to call back, or should ... call you?
Möchten Sie (vielleicht) eine Nachricht hinterlassen?	Would you like to leave a message?
Ich werde ... bitten, Sie so bald wie möglich zurückzurufen.	I'll ask ... to call you back as soon as possible.
Soll ich Sie zu seiner/ihrer Assistentin/Sekretärin durchstellen?	Can I put you through to his/her assistant/secretary?

Asking for information

Wie war Ihr Name, bitte?	What was the name again, please?
Können Sie das bitte buchstabieren?	Could you spell that for me, please?

The English alphabet and international spelling code

A	Alpha	I	India	Q	Quebec	Y	Yankee
B	Bravo	J	Juliette	R	Romeo	Z	Zulu
C	Charlie	K	Kilo	S	Sierra		
D	Delta	L	Lima	T	Tango		
E	Echo	M	Mike	U	Uniform		
F	Foxtrot	N	November	V	Victor		
G	Golf	O	Oscar	W	Whisky		
H	Hotel	P	Papa	X	X-ray		

('Z' is pronounced 'zed' in British English and 'zee' in American English.)

Könnten Sie mir bitte Ihre Fax-/Telefon-/Handynummer geben?	Can/Could you give me your fax / phone / mobile phone number, please?

Saying phone numbers

- Say the individual numbers one after the other. Say the number **0** as the letter **o** (common in British English) or **zero** (common in American and International English).

- **Never** use tens (*Zehner*), eg 'fifty-seven' for 'five – seven'.

    180723   one – eight – oh/zero – seven – two – three

- Say double and triple numbers like this:

    769955   seven – six – **double nine** – **double five**   or
                seven – six – **nine nine** – **five five**

    122246   one – **double two two** – four – six   or
                one – **two double two** – four – six   or
                one – **two two two** – four – six

Können Sie mir bitte Ihre E-Mail-Adresse geben?   Can/May I have your email address, please?

Saying email addresses

- Say words in email addresses as complete words but individual letters on their own.

    e.g.   abgreen@quicknet.com   a – b – green

- Say symbols like this:

@	at
.	dot
-	dash (or hyphen)
_	underscore
/	(forward) slash

- British firms' addresses normally end with .co.uk, said as 'dot co dot u k' ('co' rhymes with 'no'). American firms' addresses normally end with .com, said as 'dot com'.

    e.g.   s_spence@browns.com   s underscore spence at browns dot com
    james-stewart@dsg.co.uk   james dash stewart at d s g dot co dot u k

Getting out of trouble

Tut mir Leid, das habe ich nicht verstanden. Können Sie das bitte noch mal sagen?	I'm sorry, I didn't get/understand that. Could you repeat it / say it again, please?
Könnten Sie bitte etwas langsamer/lauter sprechen?	Could you speak more slowly / a little louder, please?
Einen Moment bitte. Ich verbinde Sie mit jemanden, der Englisch spricht / besser Englisch spricht als ich.	One moment, please. I'll put you through to somebody who can speak English (better than I can).

Saying goodbye

Vielen Dank für Ihren Anruf. Auf Wiederhören.	Thank you (very much) for your call. Goodbye.
Auf Wiederhören und vielen Dank für Ihre Hilfe.	Goodbye and thanks a lot / thank you (very much) for your help.

2 Arranging appointments

Asking for an appointment

Ich würde gerne einen Termin für ein Treffen mit … abmachen.	I'd like to make an appointment to see …, please.
Wäre es möglich, dass ich … treffe?	Would it be possible for me to see …, please?

Fixing a time and date

Haben Sie ein bestimmtes Datum im Kopf?	Do you have any particular date in mind?
Wie wäre es mit (10 Uhr) am / nächsten / kommenden (Mittwoch) / am (15.)?	How/What about (10 o'clock) on / next / this coming (Wednesday) / on (the 15th)?

Würde Ihnen (10 Uhr) / nächsten / kommenden (Mittwoch) / am (15.) passen?	Would (10 o'clock) on / next / this coming (Wednesday) on (the 15th) be all right / convenient?

Saying dates

written	spoken	
6 June 2005 6th June 2005	the sixth of June, two thousand and five	(usual in British English)
June 6, 2005 June 6th, 2005	June (the) sixth, two thousand-five	(usual in American English)

Accepting and rejecting suggestions

Kein Problem. (12.30 Uhr) am / nächsten / kommenden (Dienstag) / am (23.) passt mir / ist in Ordnung.	No problem. (12.30) on / next / this coming (Tuesday) / on (the 23rd) will suit me fine / very well.
Ja, (12.30 Uhr) am/nächsten (Dienstag) / am (23.) würde ich schaffen.	Yes, I can make it by (12.30) on / next (Tuesday) / on (the 23rd).
Da hat ... leider eine Besprechung / einen anderen Termin.	I'm afraid ... has a meeting / another appointment then.
Leider ist ... dann nicht hier / auf Dienstreise / in Urlaub.	Unfortunately, ... is not here / on a business trip / on holiday then.

Closing

Schön. Dann freue ich mich / freuen wir uns Sie am (Mittwoch dem 22.) zu treffen.	Fine. I'll/We'll look forward to seeing you on (Wednesday the 22nd), then.
Gut. Dann erwarten wir Sie um 16 Uhr am (Mittwoch dem 22.).	Good. We'll expect you at (4pm) on (Wednesday the 22nd).

Office communication: telephoning   UNIT 2   21

 Practising language

1 Use the English alphabet to dictate these abbreviations to your partner. Swap roles at least once. Then match each group of abbreviations with a category from the box.

1 AA[1] – BA[2] – KLM[3] – SAS[4] – TWA[5]
2 ABC[1] – ARD[2] – BBC[3] – CNN[4] – RTL[5]
3 BASF[1] – BMW[2] – GMC[3] – IBM[4] – MAN[5] – VAG[6]
4 ISO[1] – NAFTA[2] – UN[3] – WTO[4] – WWF[5]

> airlines
> broadcasters
> international organisations
> manufacturers

2 First, read the model dialogue below to see how to spell out names. Then use the English alphabet and the international spelling code (*see page 18*) to role-play the dialogue with a partner using names from the box. Swap roles at least once.

You   Can you tell me your last name, please?
Partner Of course. It's Hughes.
You   Could you spell that for me, please?
Partner Sure. It's H – U – G – H – E – S.
You   Sorry, is that 'S' for Sierra?
Partner That's right.
You   Thanks, Ms Hughes.

> Mr Hidvegi   Mr Ogunyemi
> Ms Kepuska   Ms Piatkowski
> Mr Laroussi   Mr Rozendaal
> Ms Müller (ue)   Ms Steinmaier

3 Read the sentences to your partner, who should note down the phone numbers. Swap roles at least once.

1 My number's 0044 for the UK, then 141 for Glasgow, then 678 8430.
2 You can reach me on my mobile. The number's 0164, then 6453682.
3 The number of my hotel is 0221 for Cologne, then 723132.
4 We've moved. Our new number is 07531 for Constance, then 189707.
5 Can you fax confirmation, please? The number's 0031 for the Netherlands, then 182 for Gouda, then 330061.
6 You can phone Rolf direct on 030 for Berlin, then 8978584-09.

4 Dictate the email and website addresses to your partner. Swap roles at least once.

1 info@ifabs.co.uk
2 oduval@wanadoo.fr
3 anton.riedesel@aon.at
4 www.bbc.co.uk/radio4
5 www.save-whales.org
6 www.hrs.com

5 Dictate the dates to your partner. Only give the year when necessary. Swap roles once.

EXAMPLE: the date of the reunification of Germany
          the third of October, nineteen-ninety

1 today's date
2 your date of birth
3 the date you last went to the cinema
4 the date of your last English test
5 the date of the next public holiday
6 a date that you will never forget

UNIT 2 Office communication: telephoning

6 **What would you say in English in these situations? Put in any missing names or dates yourself.**

Sie möchten jemanden fragen bzw. jemandem sagen,

1 ... ob Sie einen Termin haben können, um (Name) zu besuchen.
2 ... wie es mit (Uhrzeit) am nächsten (Tag) / am (Datum) wäre.
3 ... ob die Person, die Sie besuchen wollen, selbst einen Termin vorschlagen möchte.
4 ... dass (Name) am (Tag) verreist ist.
5 ... dass die andere Person Anfang nächste Woche nochmals anrufen soll.
6 ... dass Sie am (Tag) schon voll ausgebucht sind.

Listening comprehension

7 **Listen to the dialogue. Which of the following expressions do you hear? Each time only one of the two items is correct.**

1 a How may I help you?
  b Can I help you?

2 a Can you put me through to ...?
  b May I speak to ...?

3 a May I ask who's speaking, please?
  b Who's calling, please?

4 a Hold the line, please.
  b I'll just put you through.

5 a May I speak to ...?
  b Is ... there, please?

6 a I'm afraid ... is busy at the moment.
  b I'm afraid ... is in a meeting at the moment.

7 a I'll call again later.
  b I'll ring again tomorrow.

8 a Would you like to leave a message?
  b Can I take a message?

Now put the other expressions from above into the following dialogue. Two of the items do not fit at all.

Geoff Good afternoon. Smith and Co. ...[1]?

Julia Good afternoon. Can I speak to Mr Smith, please?

Geoff ...[2]?

Julia It's Julia Gordon from Kramer Ltd.

Geoff ...[3], Ms Gordon.

Sarah Good afternoon. Mr Smith's office. Sarah Jones speaking.

Julia Hello. This is Julia Gordon from Kramer Ltd. Is Mr Smith there, please?

Sarah ...[4]. But he should be free at about 3 o'clock. ...[5]?

Julia Could you tell him I called and ...[6], please?

Sarah Of course. Bye.

Julia Goodbye.

Office communication: telephoning UNIT 2 23

D Role-playing

1 Translate Bernd's part of the conversation into English and then role-play it with a partner.

It is a Saturday afternoon. Bernd Katthöfer is in London on a business trip. He is phoning Jason Ross, a British businessman.

Mary Hello.
Bernd *Em... ist das Ipswich 57332, bitte?*
Mary Yes, that's right. Mary Ross speaking.
Bernd *Guten Morgen, Frau Ross. Mein Name ist Bernd Katthöfer aus Deutschland. Kann ich bitte Ihren Mann sprechen?*
Mary Oh, dear. I'm afraid he's not in at the moment. But can I give him a message?
Bernd *Das ist sehr nett von Ihnen, aber eigentlich wollte ich mit ihm persönlich sprechen. Als wir uns neulich bei der CeBit in Hannover kennen gelernt haben, hat er mich gebeten, ihn anzurufen, wenn ich in England bin. Kann ich ihn vielleicht per Handy erreichen?*
Mary Well, not really. He's playing in a tennis match in Cambridge today, you see.
Bernd *Ich verstehe. Kann ich heute abend wieder anrufen, gegen halb neun?*
Mary No problem. I won't be at home myself, but I'll leave a note for Jason by the telephone. Could I have your name again, please?
Bernd *Natürlich. Mein Name ist Katthöfer. Bernd Katthöfer.*
Mary Oh, dear. Could you spell that for me, please?
Bernd *Sicher. (Er buchstabiert seinen Nachnamen mit 'oe' für 'ö'.)*
Mary Fine, I've got that. Well, thank you for your call, Mr Katthöfer, and I'll make sure Jason gets your message. Goodbye.
Bernd *Auf Wiederhören, Frau Ross und vielen Dank für Ihre Hilfe.*

2 Work with a partner. Use suitable telephone language to role-play the conversation. Put your chairs back to back. Make notes first, adding suitable names, polite forms etc.

A ruft bei B's Firma an, um eine bestimmte Person zu sprechen.

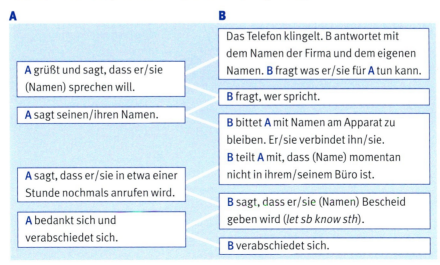

E Unit word list

Page 14	to arrange an appointment	*einen Termin abmachen*
	to put sb through	*jdn. durchstellen*
	to be available	*erreichbar sein*
	to fix a date/time	*ein(e) Datum/Zeit festlegen*
	to exaggerate	*übertreiben*
	countless	*zahllos*
	global economy	*Weltwirtschaft*
	to leave a message	*eine Nachricht hinterlassen*
	to market	*verkaufen, vertreiben*
	range (of products)	*Sortiment, Produktpalette*
	embassy	*Botschaft*
	specialist	*Fach-*
	consultancy	*Beratung*
	experienced	*erfahren*
	joint owner	*Mitbesitzer*
Page 15	to take a message	*etw. ausrichten*
	to pronounce	*aussprechen*
	to hold the line	*am Apparat bleiben*
Page 16	(trade) fair	*Messe*
	venue	*(Veranstaltungs)Ort*
	conference centre	*Konferenzzentrum*
	exhibition ground	*Messegelände*
	to be signed	*ausgeschildert sein*
Page 21	to dictate	*diktieren*
	abbreviation	*Abkürzung*
	category	*Kategorie*
	broadcaster	*Rundfunk-/Fernsehanstalt*
	reunification	*Wiedervereinigung*
Page 22	to be free	*verfügbar sein, Zeit haben*
Useful words	extension number	*Durchwahl*
	engaged	*besetzt*
	to repeat	*wiederholen*
	to be on another line	*auf einer anderen Leitung sprechen*

Office communication: emails

Model emails: making and confirming appointments, making and confirming hotel reservations, invitations and thank-you letters

Useful phrases: making appointments; making hotel reservations; invitations and thank-you letters

When to write emails

Most business correspondence deals with routine business matters, such as buying and selling. However, correspondence dealing with things like appointments, travel arrangements or hotel accommodation also needs to be sent, generally as emails. Unlike business letters, emails make use of spoken language, i.e. **short forms** (*it's, hasn't, we'd*) and an informal style, e.g. *Please let us know ...* rather than *We would be grateful if you could advise us ...* In fact, if you want to use a more formal style, then it is better so send a letter.

How to write emails

Salutation	*Good morning/afternoon*, (Name)	standard
	Dear (Name)	quite formal
	Hello/Hi (Name)	informal, particularly *Hi*
Subject	Say clearly what the email is about, for example, *I'm just writing about ...* If you are answering an email, say something like *Thank you / Thanks for your email about ...*	
Close	Thank the other person for his or her trouble/help, or say that you hope the arrangements you have made are satisfactory. Always ask the other person to get in touch if necessary.	
Signing off	*Yours sincerely/faithfully* sounds too formal in emails. Write something like *Best regards/wishes*, *All the best* or simply *Yours*.	

The situation

Kent Casings Limited is a British manufacturer of clear plastic cases for CDs, DVDs and video games. It is situated in Ashford in Kent, not far from the tunnel terminal at Cheriton.

Plastex GmbH in Zwickau is a German manufacturer of advanced plastics. It supplies Kent Casings with plastics for many of its products.

Kate Medway is head of purchasing at Kent Casings. She often deals with Plastex. *Joe Davis* is Kate's personal assistant or 'PA'.

Rolf Schubert is the export manager at Plastex. Kent Casings is one of his biggest customers, so he and his secretary, *Julia Graf*, have a lot of contact with Kate and Joe.

A Model emails

1 Making and confirming appointments

Julia Graf and Joe Davis are arranging for Julia's boss, Rolf Schubert, to visit Kate Medway in Ashford.

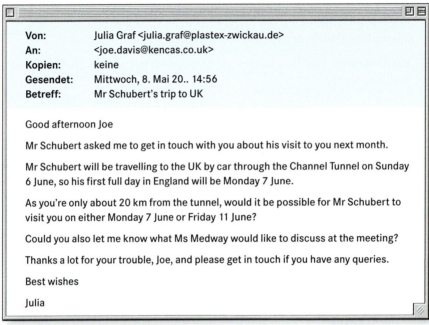

Von:	Julia Graf <julia.graf@plastex-zwickau.de>
An:	<joe.davis@kencas.co.uk>
Kopien:	keine
Gesendet:	Mittwoch, 8. Mai 20.. 14:56
Betreff:	Mr Schubert's trip to UK

Good afternoon Joe

Mr Schubert asked me to get in touch with you about his visit to you next month.

Mr Schubert will be travelling to the UK by car through the Channel Tunnel on Sunday 6 June, so his first full day in England will be Monday 7 June.

As you're only about 20 km from the tunnel, would it be possible for Mr Schubert to visit you on either Monday 7 June or Friday 11 June?

Could you also let me know what Ms Medway would like to discuss at the meeting?

Thanks a lot for your trouble, Joe, and please get in touch if you have any queries.

Best wishes

Julia

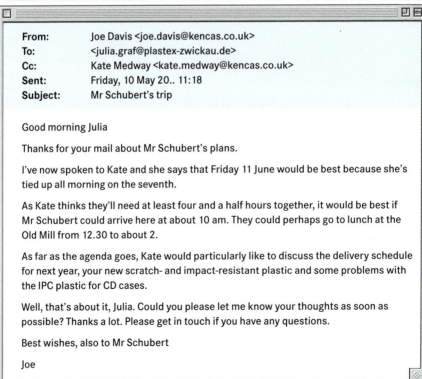

From:	Joe Davis <joe.davis@kencas.co.uk>
To:	<julia.graf@plastex-zwickau.de>
Cc:	Kate Medway <kate.medway@kencas.co.uk>
Sent:	Friday, 10 May 20.. 11:18
Subject:	Mr Schubert's trip

Good morning Julia

Thanks for your mail about Mr Schubert's plans.

I've now spoken to Kate and she says that Friday 11 June would be best because she's tied up all morning on the seventh.

As Kate thinks they'll need at least four and a half hours together, it would be best if Mr Schubert could arrive here at about 10 am. They could perhaps go to lunch at the Old Mill from 12.30 to about 2.

As far as the agenda goes, Kate would particularly like to discuss the delivery schedule for next year, your new scratch- and impact-resistant plastic and some problems with the IPC plastic for CD cases.

Well, that's about it, Julia. Could you please let me know your thoughts as soon as possible? Thanks a lot. Please get in touch if you have any questions.

Best wishes, also to Mr Schubert

Joe

a Answer the questions about the first email.

1 Who is the email from, and who is it to? When was the email sent?
2 How is Mr Schubert travelling to England?
3 Why does Mr Schubert want to visit Ashford on either his first or last day in England?
4 Apart from fixing a date, what other information does the sender ask for?

b Say if the statements about the second email are true (T), false (F) or you can't say because the information is not given in the email (–). Correct the false sentences.

1 Kate is in a planning meeting all morning on Monday.
2 Kate thinks she'll need about four and a half hours with Mr Schubert.
3 Kate says Mr Schubert can come at any time he wants on 11 June.
4 Kate and Mr Schubert will have lunch in the staff canteen.
5 Joe is joining Kate and Mr Schubert for lunch at the Old Mill.
6 Kate wants to talk about breakage problems with IPC plastic.

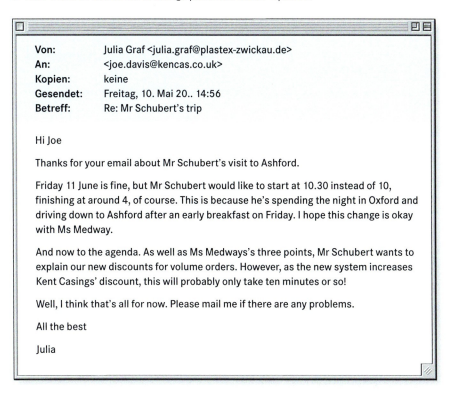

Von:	Julia Graf <julia.graf@plastex-zwickau.de>
An:	<joe.davis@kencas.co.uk>
Kopien:	keine
Gesendet:	Freitag, 10. Mai 20.. 14:56
Betreff:	Re: Mr Schubert's trip

Hi Joe

Thanks for your email about Mr Schubert's visit to Ashford.

Friday 11 June is fine, but Mr Schubert would like to start at 10.30 instead of 10, finishing at around 4, of course. This is because he's spending the night in Oxford and driving down to Ashford after an early breakfast on Friday. I hope this change is okay with Ms Medway.

And now to the agenda. As well as Ms Medways's three points, Mr Schubert wants to explain our new discounts for volume orders. However, as the new system increases Kent Casings' discount, this will probably only take ten minutes or so!

Well, I think that's all for now. Please mail me if there are any problems.

All the best

Julia

c Complete the sentences with details from the email.

1 Mr Schubert would like to start at … ^{1} am instead of … ^{2} am because he is driving to … ^{3} from … ^{4}.
2 … ^{1} would also like to talk about Plastex's new discounts for … ^{2} orders.
3 … ^{1} does not think Mr Schubert will need more than about … ^{2} minutes because the new … ^{3} increases Kent Casings' … ^{4}.

2 Making and confirming hotel reservations

Kate Medway has offered to find Mr Schubert a hotel for his visit and has asked Joe to book a room. The email is to The Garden House in Marsham confirming a telephone reservation.

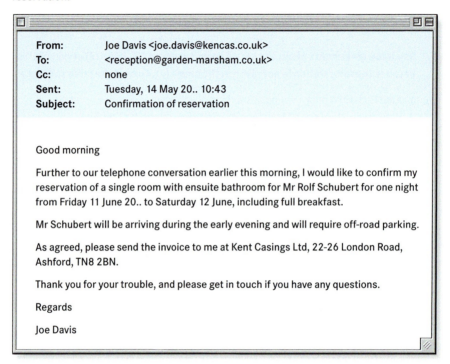

Join sentence parts 1–8 with a–j to make true statements. Two items in list a–j do not fit at all.

1 Before closing, Joe told the hotel
2 He agreed with the hotel that the invoice
3 Joe asked for a full breakfast
4 Joe Davis sent an email to
5 Joe had telephoned the hotel reception
6 Joe told the hotel that the guest
7 The purpose of the email was
8 The reservation was for a single

a earlier on the same morning.
b Julia in answer to her query about parking.
c room for one night for Rolf Schubert.
d The Garden House on 14 May.
e to be included in the price of the room.
f to confirm a telephone reservation.
g to contact him if there were any queries.
h to let him know about conference facilities.
i would also require off-road parking.
j would be sent to him at Kent Casings.

3 Invitations and thank-you letters

In this email, Rolf Schubert invites Kate Medway to have dinner with him on his last evening in England.

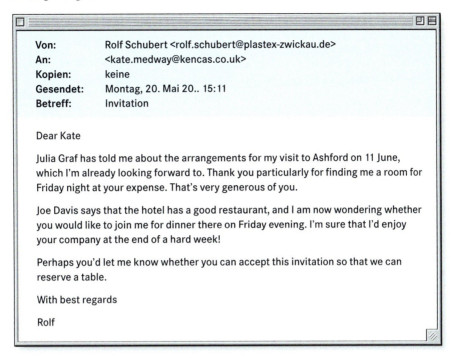

Von:	Rolf Schubert <rolf.schubert@plastex-zwickau.de>
An:	<kate.medway@kencas.co.uk>
Kopien:	keine
Gesendet:	Montag, 20. Mai 20.. 15:11
Betreff:	Invitation

Dear Kate

Julia Graf has told me about the arrangements for my visit to Ashford on 11 June, which I'm already looking forward to. Thank you particularly for finding me a room for Friday night at your expense. That's very generous of you.

Joe Davis says that the hotel has a good restaurant, and I am now wondering whether you would like to join me for dinner there on Friday evening. I'm sure that I'd enjoy your company at the end of a hard week!

Perhaps you'd let me know whether you can accept this invitation so that we can reserve a table.

With best regards

Rolf

In this email, Kate accepts Rolf's dinner invitation.

Good afternoon, Rolf

Many thanks for your kind invitation to have dinner with you at The Garden House on Friday 11 June, which I'm delighted to accept. I'm already looking forward to it!

I hope you'll let me return your generosity when I visit you in Zwickau in the autumn.

All the best

Kate

How do Rolf and Kate express these ideas in the emails? Be careful. They are not necessarily in the same order.

Rolf
1 … findet Kent Casings' Angebot, seine Hotelkosten zu übernehmen, sehr großzügig.
2 … möchte Kate gerne zum Abendessen einladen.
3 … freut sich über seinen Termin in Ashford.

Kate
4 … bedankt sich bei Rolf für die Einladung.
5 … nimmt die Einladung mit Freude an.
6 … hofft, dass sie sich für Rolfs Großzügigkeit im Herbst revanchieren kann.

B Useful phrases

1 Making appointments

Herr/Frau … würde gerne einen Termin vereinbaren, um Herrn/Frau … zu besuchen.	Mr/Ms … would like to make an appointment to visit Mr/Ms …
Wenn möglich, möchte … Sie am (23. Juni) um (17.30) besuchen.	If possible, … would like to visit you on (23 June) at (5.30pm).
Sollte dieser Termin ungünstig sein, schlagen Sie bitte ein anderes Datum vor.	Should this time be inconvenient, please suggest another date.
Da Herr/Frau … am (19. April) / vom (17.) bis (21. April) in … ist, …	As Mr/Ms … is in … on (19 April) / from (17) to (21 April), …
… würde er/sie gerne, die Gelegenheit nutzen, … zu besuchen.	… he/she would like to take the opportunity of visiting …
Er/Sie würde gerne mit … über zukünftige Geschäftsmöglichkeiten sprechen.	He/She would like to discuss future business opportunities with …
… unsere neuen Rabatte/Preise erläutern.	… explain our new/revised discounts/prices.
… Herrn/Frau … unseren neuesten Katalog überreichen.	… deliver/present our latest catalogue to Mr/Ms …
… unser neues Produkt / unsere neue Produktreihe präsentieren.	… demonstrate/present our new product (line).
… Herrn/Frau … unsere/n neue/n Außendienstmitarbeiter/in für (Gebiet) vorstellen.	… introduce our new representative for … to Mrs/Ms …

2 Making hotel reservations

Haben Sie Einzel-/Doppelzimmer (frei) für die (4) Nächte vom (3.) bis (7. November)?	Do you have any single/double rooms (free) for the (4) nights from (3) to (7 November)?
Wir brauchen/benötigen … Zimmer für die … Nächte vom … bis …	We need/require … rooms for the … nights from … to …
Ich hätte / Wir hätten gerne … Einzel- und … Doppelzimmer mit Bad.	I/We would like … single and … double rooms with ensuite facilities.
Die Doppelzimmer sollten Doppelbetten / zwei Einzelbetten haben.	The double rooms should have double/twin beds.
Ich würde / Wir würden gerne … Zimmer für die … Nächte vom … bis … reservieren.	I'd/We'd like to reserve … rooms for the … nights from … to …
Ankunftstag ist …, Abreise am … nach dem Frühstück.	The day of arrival is … and departure will be after breakfast on …
Das/Die Zimmer sollte(n) möglichst ruhig sein.	The room(s) should be as quiet as possible.

Wir hätten gerne / benötigen Parkplätze in der Garage / auf dem Hotelparkplatz für (4) PKWs / Fahrzeuge.	We would like/require spaces in the hotel garage / car park for (4) cars/vehicles.
Ich benötige / Wir benötigen ebenfalls einen Konferenzraum / Konferenzräume für (25) Teilnehmer/innen / Personen.	I/We will also require a conference room / conference rooms for (25) participants/ people.
Das Konferenzzimmer sollte mit einem/einer Beamer/Tageslichtprojektor/Flipchart/Internetverbindung/ ... ausgestattet sein.	The conference room should be equipped with a video projector / an overhead projector / a flipchart / internet connection / ...
Bestätigen Sie bitte diese Reservierung per Email/Fax.	Please confirm this reservation by email/fax.
Schicken Sie bitte die Rechnung an (Firma) zu Händen von ...	Please send the invoice to ... for the attention of ...
Die Firma ... wird alle Kosten begleichen außer den Kosten für Bar-/Minibar-/Telefon-/Bezahlfernsehen.	... will meet all costs except for those for the bar / minibar / phone calls / pay-TV.

3 Invitations and thank-you letters

Ich möchte / Wir möchten Sie zu einem Empfang / zu der Einweihung unserer neuen Geschäftsstelle / zum Abendessen am ... in ... einladen.	I/We would like to invite you to a reception / the opening of our new branch / dinner at / in ... on ...
Ich freue mich / Wir freuen uns (sehr), Sie zu ... am ... in ... einzuladen.	I/We have (great) pleasure in inviting you to ... at ... on ...
Die Feierlichkeiten beginnen / Der Empfang beginnt um ... und wird circa ... Stunden dauern.	The celebrations/reception begin(s) at ... and will last about ... hours.
Wir würden uns freuen, Sie am ... zu ... begrüßen zu dürfen und hoffen (sehr), dass Sie diese Einladung annehmen können.	We would be delighted to welcome you to ... on ... and (very much) hope that you will be able to accept this invitation.
Vielen Dank für Ihre freundliche Einladung zu ... am ..., die ich/wir (sehr) gerne annehmen.	Thank you very much (indeed) for your kind invitation to ... on ..., which I/we are delighted to / would like to accept.
... leider wegen einer Geschäftsreise / einer anderen Verpflichtung nicht annehmen kann/können.	... am/are unfortunately unable to accept because of a business trip / a prior engagement.
Vielen Dank für einen (sehr) angenehmen Tag/ Nachmittag/Abend, den ich/wir sehr genossen habe/haben.	Many thanks for a (very) pleasant day/ afternoon/evening, which I/we enjoyed very much.

C Practising language

1 Complete the email about a change to a room reservation with words or expressions from the box. Be careful. Two of the items do not fit at all.

> are | arrive | be taken | change | going | Good morning
> in touch | made | questions | regards | reservation | tomorrow | train
> until 10:50 | won't arrive | your trouble

...¹

I'm afraid that we have got to ...² the reservation we ...³ for Ms Sigrid Janssen because she isn't ...⁴ to the Bristol Marine Fair after all. Her place will now ...⁵ by Mr Klaus Beck.

All the other details of the ...⁶ stay as they ...⁷.

Just one last thing. Mr Beck ...⁸ at the hotel until about 11:30 pm as his ...⁹ from London doesn't get to Bristol ...¹⁰.

Thanks a lot for ...¹¹, and please get ...¹² if you have any ...¹³.

Best ...¹⁴

2 Take turns at reading the sentences out to a partner using the short form of the expressions in *italics*.

EXAMPLE: *I will* send out the invoice tomorrow.
I'll send out the invoice tomorrow.

1 The *letter is* in the post.
2 My *name is*[1] Sally Winters. *I am*[2] Mr Cobb's secretary.
3 *She has* been working here for ages.
4 The goods *were not* properly packed.
5 *They will*[1] visit us when *they are*[2] in London.
6 I *do not*[1] think that *you will*[2] get the job.
7 *We would*[1] do much better if we *did not*[2] have to pay so much tax.
8 I *have not*[1] seen Jane all week. She *is not*[2] ill, is she?
9 You *must not* talk to customers like that.
10 *I have*[1] heard that Tony *will not*[2] be at the meeting.

Office communication: emails UNIT **3** 33

3 **Choose which of the two words or expressions in *italics* would be more suitable for an email. Don't forget that in emails we use informal spoken language.**

You asked me to *let you know / inform you* [1] when our marketing manager, Mr Peter Baxter, *envisages visiting / plans to visit* [2] Canada with a view to *arranging / fixing* [3] a meeting.

Mr Baxter's *itinerary is / travel plans are* [4] now *essentially / more or less* [5] finalised, and he'll be in Montreal for two full days, arriving on 11 March and *departing / leaving* [6] again for Detroit, where he is *attending / going to* [7] the spring automotive fair, early on 14 March. He *flies back / returns by air* [8] to the UK on the seventeenth.

As / Due to the fact that [9] Mr Baxter would very much like to meet Mr O'Neill, he is *considering / wondering* [10] whether either the morning of 13 or 14 March would be *convenient / okay* [11]. The meeting *could / might* [12] take place either at Mr Baxter's hotel, the Monarch, or at Mr O'Neill's office, of course.

Could you please let me know which of the two dates would be *best / most suitable* [13] and where the meeting could take place? As *things are / this matter is* [14] now *becoming / getting* [15] rather urgent, I'd be glad of *an early / a prompt* [16] reply.

Thank you very much / Very many thanks [17] for your *efforts / trouble* [18], and I look forward to hearing from you. Please *don't hesitate to contact us / let us know* [19] if you have any *queries / questions* [20].

4 **This email confirming a room reservation is complete, but the parts are mixed up. Arrange the email in the proper order.**

a I also wish to book a space in the hotel garage. Ms Klein's car is a VW Passat, registration number EN-UU 107.

b Good afternoon

c I'd like to reserve a single room with ensuite facilities for two nights, as follows:

d Best regards

e Please note that Ms Klein won't arrive at the hotel before about 10.30 pm on 6 June.

f Guest   Ms Birgit Klein
   Arrival   06 June 20..
   Departure   08 June 20..

g This is to confirm the phone reservation I made this morning.

h Thank you for your trouble, and please get in touch with me if you have any questions.

5 Study the bar chart and complete the sentences with details from the chart.

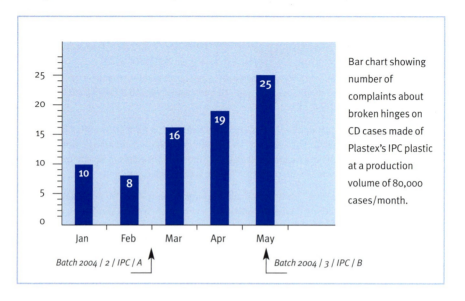

1 The complaints are about ... on CD cases made of ... .
2 Kent Casings started using Batch 2004/2/IPC/A at the beginning of ... .
3 In January, there were ... complaints, the normal number with a production volume of ... cases per ... .
4 There's an ... in complaints of over 200% between February and ... .
5 There are ... complaints in April. That's almost ... the amount there were in January.
6 Batch 2004/.../IPC/... started to be used in the ... of May.

Listening comprehension

6 Listen to Joe's phone conversation with Kim Cameron of Star Car Hire and complete his notes. Then write an email to Kate with the details.

Name (Company / Person): *Star Car Hire / Kim Cameron*

Pick up date / place:

Return date / place:

Type of car:

Price:

Extra details: *Petrol ...*

Office communication: emails   UNIT 3   35

D Writing emails

1 Work with a partner. One of you is **A**, the other **B**. Exchange emails based on the following German prompts (*Stichpunkte*). Think up names, missing details, polite forms etc. yourselves.

Email 1: A will **B** in seinem/ihrem Büro in (*Ort*) besuchen. **A** schlägt Montag, den 2. Juni, um (*Zeit*) vor, wenn er/sie sowieso in (*Ort*) sein wird. Er/Sie hofft, dass dieser Vorschlag in Ordnung ist. **Email 2: B** fragt, ob **A** zwei Stunden später kommen könnte, da er/sie vorher eine Sitzung hat. **Email 3: A** erwidert, dass der spätere Termin in Ordnung ist.

2 Work with a partner. **A** writes an email based on the note. **B** confirms the reservation.

> Vergiss bitte nicht, das York Hotel anzumailen: Einzelzimmer mit Bad / Frühstück, 8.–10. Aug. (mit Garagenplatz). Auch Tisch für 4 Pers. am 9. reservieren.
> Sag bitte unbedingt, dass ich am 8. voraussichtlich sehr spät ankomme (etwa um Mitternacht). Danke.

3 Work with a partner as in **1** above. Exchange emails according to the prompts.

A ist Büroangestellte/r, **B** arbeitet an der Rezeption. **Email 1: A** will ein Einzelzimmer für (*Zahl*) Nächte vom (*Datum*) bis zum (*Datum*) für (*Name*) reservieren. Er/Sie fügt hinzu, dass (*Name*) auch einen ruhigen Hund mitbringen will. **Email 2: B** bestätigt die Reservierung mit dem Hinweis, dass a) nur kleine bis mittelgroße (*medium-sized*) Hunde erlaubt sind, b) es einen Preisaufschlag (*surcharge*) von £5 pro Tag gibt und c) Hunde nicht in den Frühstücksraum mitgenommen werden dürfen.

4 Write an email based on the following note.

> Bitte Email an Mr. Carlos L. Gonzales schicken. Sagen Sie ihm, dass unser Treffen morgen, 6.11. in Ordnung geht. Ich komme ca. 9 Uhr an und werde im Foyer seines Hotels auf ihn warten. (Ich trage einen schwarzen Mantel mit rotem Schal!) Wir werden etwa 4 Stunden benötigen. Anschließend würde ich ihn gerne zum Mittagessen im Caledonian Grill einladen. Bitte sagen Sie ihm, dass ich spätestens 15.30 Uhr weg muss (Flug). Danke!
> PS: Bitte auch per Email einen Tisch reservieren!

5 You are Carlos Gonzales. Write an answer to the email in Exercise 4 as follows.

Bedanken Sie sich bei (*Name*) für ein angenehmes und produktives Gespräch. Drücken Sie Ihre Überzeugung aus, dass Ihre Firmen eine gewinnbringende Geschäftsbeziehung aufbauen werden. Bedanken Sie sich auch für das Mittagessen, das Sie sehr genossen haben. Sie hoffen, dass (*Name*) einen guten Flug hatte und freuen sich ihn/sie im Frühling bei Ihnen in Los Angeles zu sehen.

UNIT 3 Office communication: emails

E Unit word list

Page 25	to make an appointment / a hotel reservation	*einen Termin vereinbaren / ein Zimmer im Hotel reservieren lassen*
	to confirm an appointment / a hotel reservation	*einen Termin / eine Reservierung bestätigen*
	invitation; to invite	*Einladung; einladen*
	travel arrangements	*Reisepläne*
	to get in touch with so.	*sich bei jdm. melden*
	to deal with	*verhandeln mit*
	personal assistant (PA)	*persönliche/r Assistent/in*
Page 26	to arrange	*vereinbaren, ausmachen*
	to be tied up	*beschäftigt sein, zu tun haben*
	as far as … goes / is concerned	*was … betrifft / angeht*
	agenda	*Tagesordnung*
	to let so. know, to inform	*jdm. Bescheid sagen, informieren*
Page 27	to fix a date	*ein Datum festlegen*
	staff	*Mitarbeiter, Personal*
	breakage; to break	*Bruch; zerbrechen*
	discount	*Rabatt*
	volume order	*Großauftrag*
Page 28	further to	*in Bezug auf*
	ensuite bathroom	*Zimmer mit Bad*
	off-road parking	*Parkmöglichkeiten abseits der Straße*
	conference facilities; conference room	*Tagungsmöglichkeiten; Konferenzraum*
Page 29	at your expense	*auf Ihre Kosten*
	to accept an invitation	*eine Einladung annehmen*
	to return so.'s generosity	*jds. Großzügigkeit erwidern*
Page 32	properly	*richtig, gut*
	tax	*Steuern*
Page 33	to envisage	*hier: vorhaben*
	with a view to	*mit der Absicht zu …*
	itinerary	*(Reise)Route*
	essentially	*im Wesentlichen*
	to finalise	*endgültig festlegen*
	to attend	*teilnehmen an*
	due to	*aufgrund*
	to consider	*erwägen*
	to wonder	*überlegen, sich fragen*
	convenient	*günstig, passend*
	(trade) fair	*Messe*
	don't hesitate to contact me	*wenden Sie sich ruhig an mich*
Page 34	hinge	*Scharnier*
	complaint	*Beschwerde*
Useful words	to postpone an appointment	*einen Termin verlegen*
	in the week commencing …	*in der Woche vom …*
	single/double room	*Einzel-/Doppelzimmer*
	full/half board	*Voll-/Halbpension*

4 Enquiries

Model phone call, fax and letter: a general enquiry, a specific enquiry

Useful phrases: opening; background; request; close

What is an enquiry?

- There are two main kinds of enquiry: **general enquiries** and **specific enquiries**.
- The first asks for **general information** about a company's products, often in the form of a request for current catalogues, price-lists etc.
- A **specific enquiry** asks for an offer (for goods) or a quotation (for services).
  It gives exact details of the product or service required, including such information as order/model number and quantity. It may also give details of the customer's delivery requirements.

How to write enquiries

Enquiries have three or four parts, as follows:

Opening	If you are writing to a company for the first time, say where you got the firm's name and address from (see box) and who you are. If you are writing to a company you already do business with, start with giving a reason for the enquiry (see below).
Reason	Always say why you are making the enquiry. It can also be quite useful to give brief background information here.
Request	Say what you want the addressee to do. Make sure that you include all the necessary details. If you have any questions about discounts or delivery, for example, ask them here.
Close	Make a polite and friendly closing comment that motivates the addressee to answer your enquiry promptly

Where buyers find suppliers	
advertisement	We were interested to see your advertisement in *Export Focus*.
buyers' guide	We saw your entry in the *Universal Buyers' Guide*.
internet	Searching the internet, we were directed to your website.
recommendation	You were recommended to us by a customer, Carr & Sons of York.
trade fair	We visited your stand at the Medica trade fair in Düsseldorf.
trade organisation	The Chamber of Commerce in Leeds gave us your name.

UNIT 4 Enquiries

Model phone call, fax and letter

 1 Model phone call: a general enquiry

Style Four Limited in London is looking for a supplier of stretch denim for its new range of S4F designer jeans. In this dialogue, Style Four's buyer, Jane Adams, is telephoning Textil Dorn GmbH in Düsseldorf.

a Listen to the dialogue and fill in the missing information.

1 The caller's name is Jane …
2 The phone call is answered by …
3 Jane wants to speak to somebody in …
4 Pia puts Jane through to Mr …
5 Jane asks if Textil Dorn can supply …[1] cloth for …[2]
6 Specifically, Jane is interested in …[1] denim in different …[2]
7 Jane wants to see …[1] of …[2] denim.
8 Mr Dorn offers to send Jane his … of samples.

b Answer the questions with *Yes/No* + short answer.

EXAMPLE: Does Textil Dorn have an export department?
           No, it doesn't.

1 Does Mr Dorn speak good English?
2 Does Jane speak German?
3 Is Textil Dorn a manufacturers' agent?
4 Does Jane ask about denim for jeans?
5 Is the denim for the new winter collection?
6 Can Textil Dorn offer an excellent range of Italian denim?
7 Does Jane want to see samples in two colours?
8 Will Jane fax the details?

c Ask about the underlined parts.

EXAMPLE: We can supply <u>samples in six colours</u>.
           What can you supply?

1 <u>Yes</u>, I speak English.
2 I'd like to speak to <u>someone from export</u>.
3 I work for <u>Style 4 in London</u>.
4 Style 4 are looking for <u>denim cloth for jeans</u>.
5 We are manufacturing <u>a new range of jeans</u> at the moment.
6 We want some light stretch denim <u>for our summer collection</u>.
7 Textil Dorn can supply <u>black, white and dark blue</u> denim material.
8 Mr Dorn is faxing the details <u>because it is quicker than sending them by post</u>.

2 Model fax: a general enquiry

Style 4 Limited

62 Albert Street
London E1 5RT

Tel +44-(0)20-17 93 77
Fax +44-(0)20-17 93 88
Email info@styfo.co.uk
Internet www.styfo.co.uk

Facsimile *message*

To:	Textil Dorn GmbH	Date:	22 November 20..
Fax no:	+40-211-783412	Re:	enquiry
For:	Mr Jens Dorn	Pages:	1

Dear Mr Dorn

Enquiry about denim

Further to our telephone conversation today, we would be obliged if you could send us samples of the high-quality light stretch denim for our new range of designer jeans that we discussed.

Could you please also forward us three copies each of your current catalogue and price-lists as well as details of your discounts for volume orders?

Thank you very much for your trouble, and as soon as we have examined and evaluated the samples for our purposes we will get in touch with you further.

Yours sincerely

Jane Adams
Purchasing

If you have not received the number of pages shown above,
please contact us on +44-(0)20-17249377 at once.

Answer the questions with *Yes/No* + short answer as in 1b above.

1 Are Style 4's offices in Bristol?
2 Does Jane ask for an image brochure?
3 Have Jane and Mr Dorn done business before?
4 Does Jane work in the export department?

3 Model letter: a specific enquiry

Style Limited
62 Albert Street
London E1 5RT

Tel +44-(0)20-17 93 77
Fax +44-(0)20-17 93 88
Email info@styfo.co.uk
Internet www.styfo.co.uk

Textil Dorn GmbH
Karlstraße 10
40593 Düsseldorf
Germany

10 December 20..

Dear Mr Dorn

Enquiry about denim

Thank you for reacting to our request for cloth samples so promptly, and having examined them, we are pleased to advise you that they appear to fulfil our requirements in every way.

We would therefore be grateful if you could submit a firm offer according to the following details:

1. eight (8) rolls, light stretch denim, blue, LSD 873B
2. four (4) rolls, medium stretch denim, black, MSD 728BK
3. as 2 above, white, MSD 728W

Please note that all prices quoted should include transport and delivery to our London premises.

Thank you for your trouble, and we look forward to receiving a competitive offer.

Yours sincerely

Style Four Limited

[signature]

Link the words 1–8 with the definitions a–h.

1 agent
2 buyer
3 current
4 discount
5 (to) examine
6 quotation
7 sample
8 volume

a example
b (to) look at carefully
c large number
d lower price for trade buyers
e offer to supply a service on certain terms
f firm or person that acts for another firm or person
g purchaser
h up-to-date

B Useful phrases

1 Opening

Ihrem Eintrag in (Einkaufsführer) entnehmen wir, dass ...	We see from your entry in ... that ...
Wir entnehmen Ihrer Anzeige in ... vom ..., dass ...	We note from your advertisement in ... of ... that ...
Auf Ihrem Stand bei der (Ort)-Messe haben wir mit Interesse gesehen, dass ...	When we visited your stand at the ... trade fair, we were interested to see that ...
Wir entnehmen Ihrer Verkaufsbroschüre / Ihrem Verkaufsprospekt, dass ...	We understand from your sales brochure/ leaflet that ...
Sie wurden uns von einem gemeinsamen Kunden empfohlen, der uns mitgeteilt hat, dass ...	You have been recommended to us by a mutual customer, who informed us that ...
... Sie (Produkt) für die Freizeit-/Stahl-/... industrie herstellen/produzieren.	... you manufacture/produce ... for the leisure/steel/... industry.
... Ihre Firma (Produkt) zu konkurrenzfähigen Bedingungen liefert.	... your company supplies ... at competitive prices.
... Sie ein breites Sortiment von ... anbieten.	... you offer a wide range of ...

2 Background

Wir sind ein führender Importeur/Hersteller/ Großhändler von ...	We are a leading importer/manufacturer/ wholesaler of ...
Gegenwärtig erweitern wir unser Sortiment von ...	At present, we are extending our range of ...
Wir planen jetzt, ein(e) neue(r/s) ... auf den Markt zu bringen.	At the moment, we are planning to launch a new ...
Nächstes Jahr / In Kürze / ... bringen wir ein neues Sortiment von ... auf den Markt.	We are launching a new range of ... next year / shortly / ...
In (Land) gibt es einen wachsenden Markt für (Produkt) zu einem konkurrenzfähigen Preis.	There is a growing market in ... for ... at a competitive price.
Daher haben wir Interesse an ...	We are (therefore) interested in ...
Aus diesem Grund sind wir an ... interessiert.	For this reason, we are in the market for ...

3 Request

Schicken Sie uns bitte Ihren neuen/neuesten Katalog und die aktuelle Preisliste.	Please send us your new/latest catalogue and current price-list.
Bitte geben Sie Ihre Preise netto/brutto an.	Please quote your prices net/gross.
Schicken Sie uns bitte ... Muster Ihrer/s ... zur Ansicht.	Please send us ... samples/specimens of your ... for our inspection.
Würden Sie bitte veranlassen, dass Ihr/e Vertreter/in uns besucht?	Would you please arrange for your representative to visit us?
Bitte informieren Sie uns auch über Lieferzeiten.	We would (also) appreciate details of delivery periods.
Könnten Sie uns (auch) Informationen über Handels-/Mengenrabatte schicken?	Could you (also) please send us information on trade/volume discounts?
Bitte teilen Sie uns auch Einzelheiten bezüglich Ihrer Zahlungsbedingungen mit.	We would also appreciate information about your terms of payment.
Sollten Sie irgendwelche Fragen haben, setzen Sie sich bitte mit mir/uns in Verbindung.	Should you have any questions/queries, please get in touch with me/us.

4 Close

Danke im Voraus für Ihre Hilfe.	Thank you in advance for your assistance/help.
Wir freuen uns darauf, in Kürze / bald von Ihnen zu hören.	We look forward to hearing from you shortly/soon.
Über Ihre baldige Antwort würden wir uns freuen.	We would be grateful for an early reply.
Wir hoffen von Ihnen zu gegebener Zeit wieder zu hören.	We hope to hear from you again in due course.

C Practising language

1 Complete the letter with words and expressions from the box. Be careful. Three words or expressions do not fit at all.

> address | brochure | buyers | clothing | company | edition | enclosing
> faithfully | fashion | grateful | information | interested | manufacture
> ~~Request~~ | retail outlets | sale | samples | sincerely | suppliers
> testing purposes | trade discounts | trouble | zip-fasteners

Dear Sir or Madam

Request [1] for samples

We are a medium-sized German ... [2] which specializes in the ... [3] of high-quality men's ... [4] for sale through our own ... [5]. We obtained your name and ... [6] from the current ... [7] of *Fashion Trades Buyers' Guide* as ... [8] of buttons, press-studs, ... [9] and other accessories for upmarket ... [10] products.

We would be ... [11] if you could send us ... [12] of your products for ... [13]. We would also be ... [14] to hear about your ... [15] for volume orders.

Thank you for your ... [16] and we look forward to hearing from you soon.

For your own ... [17], we have pleasure in ... [18] a copy of our company image ... [19].

Yours ... [20],

(...)

2 Choose the word that fits best.

Dear Ms Adams

We are *delighted/grateful* [1] to send you our standard *offer/selection* [2] of denim *examples/samples* [3] with this letter.

We also *enclose/insert* [4] three copies of our *actual/latest* [5] catalogue and *contemporary/current* [6] price-list. You will find details of our *discounts/rebates* [7], including those for *bulk/volume* [8] orders, on the back page of the price-list. However, we are *eager/willing* [9] to discuss *special/unusual* [10] additional discounts for *periodic/regular* [11] orders.

If you have any *enquiries/queries* [12], please do not hesitate to *contact/get in touch with* [13] me.

Yours *faithfully/sincerely* [14]

(...)

3 Read the email and then match the underlined parts from the email to their more formal equivalents a–o.

I got¹ your email address off the web². Anyhow, a mate³ of mine was going through some old bike mags⁴ the other day⁵, and he saw⁶ your ad⁷ about BSA, Matchless and the rest⁸.

We're dealers in old bikes like them⁹ so we're always looking for original parts for them. For example, right now¹⁰ I'm desperate for¹¹ a fuel tank for a 1938 Matchless 500. Any chance?¹²

Can you still supply this kind of stuff?¹³ If yes,¹⁴ please give us a ring.¹⁵

a advertisement
b at present
c back numbers of motorbike magazines
d call me
e Can you help me?
f classic bikes of this type
g discovered
h friend

i from the internet
j I am urgently looking for
k If you are able to do so
l obtained
m recently
n similar makes
o type of product

4 Put the sentences of this enquiry into the correct order.

a As a supplier of tennis equipment and clothing, we are currently expanding our range and wish to start supplying women's wear as well as men's wear.
b Dear Sir or Madam
c Purchasing Manager
d Thank you in advance for your help.
e We look forward to hearing from you soon.
f We saw your advertisement in the July issue of 'Fashion World' and were particularly interested by your range of sportswear.
g Yours faithfully
h We would also appreciate information about volume and trade discounts.
i Karen McDonald
j We would, therefore, be very grateful if you could send us a copy of your brochure, as well as an up-to-date price-list.

D Writing letters

1 Use the material in the box to complete the enquiry about exercise cycles for fitness studios.

Opening
- express interest in products, refer to an advertisement in 'Health and Fitness World' magazine

Background information, reason for enquiry
- you are a Munich-based fitness-centre chain
- you are particularly interested in exercise cycles 'ProMedic'

Request
- ask for a representative to call, as well as price-lists and terms of business
- also appreciate information about discounts

Close
- thank addressee for their trouble
- look forward to hearing from them

Dear Sir or Madam

We saw your advertisement in the latest issue of 'Health and Fitness World' magazine and …

---

2 Write an enquiry from notes.

Situation: Sie arbeiten für die Firma Büromöbelzentrum-Stern GmbH (BMZS) in Wuppertal. Momentan suchen Sie Computermöbel für eine neue Ausstellungsfläche (*display space*).

Aufgabe
Schreiben Sie eine erste Anfrage an John Harris & Sons Ltd, 24 Union Road, Belfast, BT5 9HJ unter dem heutigen Datum. Benutzen Sie dabei folgende Angaben:

- BMZS ist ein auf hochwertige Computermöbel spezialisierter Großhandelsbetrieb (*wholesaler*) mit Filialen in West- und Norddeutschland.
- Sie haben die Produkte der Firma John Harris & Sons Ltd bei einer Möbelausstellung (*furniture exhibition*) in Köln kennen gelernt.
- Sie sind vor allem an dem patentierten Stehpult (*patented high desk*) für Computerbenutzer, das John Harris entwickelt hat, interessiert.
- Bitten Sie um die Zusendung von Verkaufsunterlagen (*sales literature*) und Preislisten für alle Stehpulte.
- Wenn Qualität und Preis marktgerecht sind (*in line with market requirements*), können Sie größere Aufträge in Aussicht stellen (*hold out the prospect of …*).

3 Write an email from notes.

Situation: Sie arbeiten bei der Firma Hohmann Gerätebau GmbH in Dresden. Die Firma benötigt Kabelanschlüsse (*cable connectors*) für ihre neue Serie (*range*) von leichten Heckenscheren (*hedge trimmers*).

> **Aufgabe**
> Schreiben Sie eine Anfrage in Form einer E-Mail an die Firma Deltatronic Electric Ltd, 276 Harbour Road, Singapore 659321 unter dem heutigen Datum. Verwenden Sie die folgenden Angaben:
> - Information zu Produkten/Firma aus dem Internet
> - Hohmann deutscher Hersteller hochwertiger Elektrogartengeräte (*high-quality electrical garden equipment*)
> - wasserdichte (*watertight*) Kabelanschlüsse für neue Serie Heckenscheren zu konkurrenzfähigem (*competitive*) Preis
> - Angebot: 1000 Stück WT75-Anschlüsse, Kunststoff (*plastic*), grün, Best.-Nr. WT75-029LG.
> - Lieferung: Luftfracht, CPT Flughafen Dresden.
> - unabdingbare Voraussetzung (*absolute requirement*): Erfüllung (*compliance with*) der europäischen Sicherheitsvorschriften (*safety regulations*)

4 Summarize the letter.

Situation: Sie arbeiten für die Firma Farben & Lacke Koch GmbH in Wismar und haben folgendes Schreiben von der holländischen Firma Baltus Containerbow BV in Alkmaar erhalten.

> **Aufgabe**
> Lesen Sie die Anfrage und schreiben Sie für Ihre Chefin, Frau Gisela Koch, einen Vermerk über das Schreiben in deutscher Sprache.

> **Enquiry about container coatings**
>
> Dear Sirs
>
> We are a specialist Dutch manufacturer of maritime containers based in Alkmaar in North Holland. We obtained your name and address from a mutual customer, North Sea Freight Ltd of Sunderland, UK, who informed us about your high-quality water and impact resistant coatings on their container ships.
>
> We are currently planning to produce a new range of compact watertight steel containers for ondeck transportation by freight barges because they are lighter and hence easier to handle. We are, therefore, looking for a highly durable water and impact resistant protective coating that can be applied by spraying in automatic paint plants, by hand-spraying and by brush.
>
> Coatings should be available in the full RAL colour range and conform to all relevant European and international norms, as well as the new EU environmental regulations (obligatory from 1 Jan 2006).
>
> Please supply us with 5 litre samples of each of your coatings in a selection of primary colours for technical testing. Please also send all relevant technical data sheets and application instructions.
>
> Thank you for your trouble, and we look forward to receiving the samples shortly and hopefully doing business together.
>
> Yours faithfully
> Baltus Containerbow BV
>
> Ruud van Laar
> Technical Services

E Unit word list

Page 37		
	enquiry	*Anfrage*
	current	*aktuell*
	price-list	*Preisliste*
	offer	*Angebot*
	quotation	*(Preis)Angebot*
	order/model number	*Auftrags-/Modellnummer*
	delivery (requirements)	*Lieferungserfordernisse*
	discount	*Rabatt*
	buyer's guide	*Einkaufsführer*
	recommendation; to recommend	*Empfehlung; empfehlen*
	Chamber of Commerce	*Handelskammer*
Page 38	supplier	*Lieferant*
	denim	*Jeansstoff*
	sample	*Muster, Probe(stück)*
	agent	*(Handels)Vertreter/in, Vermittler/in*
	range	*Sortiment, Angebot*
Page 39	to examine	*untersuchen, prüfen*
	to evaluate	*auswerten, beurteilen*
Page 40	to fulfil our requirements	*unseren Anforderungen entsprechen*
	to submit a (firm) offer	*ein (verbindliches) Angebot machen*
	to quote a price	*einen Preis angeben/nennen*
	to include	*enthalten*
	premises	*Geschäftsräume*
	competitive offer	*günstiges Angebot*
Page 43	retail outlet	*Einzelhandelsgeschäft*
	testing purposes	*Prüfungszwecke*
	zip-fastener	*Reißverschluss*
	medium-sized	*mittelgroß, mittelständisch*
	press-stud	*Druckknopf*
	upmarket	*anspruchsvoll*
	contemporary	*gegenwärtig*
	bulk/volume order	*Großauftrag*
	eager	*begierig, erwartungsvoll*
	additional	*Zusatz-*
	query	*Nachfrage*
Page 44	make	*Fabrikat*
	issue	*Ausgabe*
Page 45	chain	*Kette*
Page 46	based in	*ansässig in*
	to conform to	*sich richten nach*
	to do business with so.	*Geschäfte mit jdm. machen*
Useful words	sales material/literature	*Prospektmaterial, Prospekte*
	on sale or return	*mit Rückgaberecht, in Kommission*
	well-established	*gut eingeführt*
	to provide so. with	*jdm. etw. zukommen lassen*

Offers and quotations

Model letter: an offer	
Useful phrases: opening; details; terms; close	

What are offers and quotations?

Offers and quotations are both answers to a specific enquiry (see Unit 4). However, in normal usage, an **offer** relates to **goods** (*Güter*), and a **quotation** to **services** (*Dienstleistungen*).

They tell the customer on what **conditions** (price, discount, delivery, terms of payment) the seller is willing to supply the goods or services required.

In the case of 'off-the-shelf' products of no great value, **standard offers** – i.e. offers without any special terms – are generally made by simply completing a form. You will usually find the supplier's **Terms and Conditions of Business** (*Geschäftsbedingungen*) on the back of the form, often in small print. Read these carefully as they are legally part of the offer or quotation.

Offers or quotations that involve **special terms** (*Sonderbedingungen*), such as a higher discount or more generous terms of payment, can be in letter form (see below).

How to write offers or quotations

Opening	Refer to the original enquiry, with the date. You can also say what the enquiry was about.
Details	Give clear details of quantity, product, order number and price in tabular form. You can take these details from the enquiry. Depending on the product, they can also include things like colour and finish, of course.
Terms	Give clear, complete and correct information about trade discounts, volume/quantity discounts, possible cash discounts, terms of payment and means of delivery here.
Close	Thank the addressee for their enquiry and ask them to get in touch with you if they have any questions. You can also say that you would appreciate an order, but do not overdo it (*es übertreiben*).

Model letter

An offer

Karlstr. 10 · D-40593 Düsseldorf

Telefon:	+49-(0)211-78 34 11
Telefax:	+49-(0)211-78 34 12
Email:	info@textildorn.de
Internet:	www.textildorn.de

Style Four Limited
62 Albert Street
London E1 5RT

18 December 20..

Dear Ms Adams

Offer for stretch denim

Thank you for your enquiry for denim of 10 December.

We are pleased to send you the following offer:

1	eight (8) rolls à 10 m, light stretch denim, blue, LSD 873B	€ 7.50/m: € 600.00
2	four (4) rolls à 10 m, medium stretch denim, black, MSD 728BK	€ 9.50/m: € 380.00
3	as 2 above, white, MSD 728W	€ 9.50/m: € 380.00

All prices include free delivery and transport to your London premises at 62 Albert Street, London E1 5RT.
We confirm that these prices are 12.5 % below list. We are willing to offer a further cash discount of 2.5 % on the quoted price for payment in full within a fortnight of receipt of goods. The consignment will be dispatched by road from Milan immediately upon receipt of order.

Thank you for your interest, and we would be delighted to receive your order. If you have any questions, please do not hesitate to get in touch with me.

Yours sincerely

Jens Dorn

Jens Dorn

Find the English equivalents of these German words/expressions in the letter. They are not necessarily in the same order.

1 Anfrage
2 das folgende Angebot
3 Firmengelände
4 Jeansstoff
5 nach Eingang der Bestellung
6 per LKW
7 Sehr geehrte …
8 Sendung
9 Skonto
10 unter Listenpreis

B Useful words and phrases: offers and quotations

1 Opening

Danke für / Mit Bezug auf Ihre Anfrage vom …	Thank you for / With reference to / Referring to your enquiry of …
Wir beziehen uns auf Ihre Anfrage vom …	We refer to your enquiry of …
Bezug nehmend auf Ihren Anruf vom …	With reference to your telephone call of …

2 Details

… freuen wir uns, Ihnen das folgende Angebot vorlegen zu dürfen:	… we have pleasure in submitting the following offer/quotation:
Gerne schicken wir Ihnen unser Angebot wie folgt: …	We are pleased to send you our offer/ quotation, as follows: …

3 Terms

Wir sind bereit … einzuräumen/anzubieten.	We are pleased/willing to give/offer …
… einen Einführungs-/Handels-/Mengenrabatt von … % auf den Listenpreis.	… a/an introductory/trade/volume discount of … % off list price.
… % Skonto für Bezahlung/Begleichung innerhalb von … Tagen / zwei Wochen.	… a cash discount of … % for payment/ settlement within … days / a fortnight.
Alle Preise sind netto.	All prices are net.
Die Preise sind EXW/FOB Cuxhaven / CIF Tilbury / …	The prices are EXW/FOB Cuxhaven / CIF Tilbury / …
Die Lieferung erfolgt …	Delivery will be made …
Die Sendung/Ware/Bestellung wird … ausgeliefert.	The consignment/goods/order will be dispatched …
… sofort nach Erhalt der Bestellung per Luftfracht/Bahn/LKW/Seefracht …	… immediately on receipt of order by air/rail/road/sea.
… innerhalb von 7/15/… Tagen nach Erhalt der Bestellung …	… within 7/15/… days of receipt of order.
Die Zahlung sollte … erfolgen.	Payment should be made …
… im Voraus	… in advance.
… per Nachnahme	… on delivery (P/D).
… Bezahlung bei Bestellung	… cash with order (CWO).
… bei Erhalt der Sendung/Ware/ Bestellung	… on receipt of (the) consignment/goods/ order.

... gemäß unseren üblichen Geschäftsbedingungen	... according to our usual terms and conditions of business.
... innerhalb von 10/30/... Tagen nach Lieferung	... within 10/30/... days of delivery.
... durch unwiderrufliches und bestätigtes Akkreditiv	... by irrevocable and confirmed letter of credit.
Dieses Angebot ist gültig für ... Wochen/ Monate nach dem o.g. Datum.	This offer/quotation is valid for ... weeks/ months after the above date.
Dieses Angebot ist verbindlich bis 30. Juni / ...	This offer/quotation is binding/firm until 30 June / ...
Dieses Angebot ist freibleibend/unverbindlich bis 30. Juni / ...	This offer is subject to confirmation by 30 June / ...

4 Close

Danke (nochmals) für Ihr(e) Interesse/ Anfrage.	Thank you (again) for your interest/ enquiry.
Wir sind sicher, dass ...	We are sure/certain (that) ...
Wir hoffen, dass ...	We hope/trust (that) ...
... Sie mit unserem Angebot / unseren Produkten zufrieden sein werden.	... you will be satisfied with our offer/products.
... Sie von diesem vorteilhaften Angebot Gebrauch machen werden.	... you will take advantage of this offer/quotation.
Wenn Sie irgendwelche Fragen haben, ...	If you have any questions/queries, ...
Sollten Sie weitere Informationen benötigen, ...	Should you require any further information, ...
... setzen Sie sich bitte mit mir / dem/der Unterzeichner/in / uns in Verbindung.	... please contact / get in touch with me / the undersigned / us.
Wir freuen uns, mit Ihnen in Geschäftsbeziehungen zu treten.	We look forward to doing business with you.

UNIT 5 Offers and quotations

C Practising language

1 Complete the letter with the missing words from the box. Note that there are three more words than you need.

> business | cash discount | customers | depending | discounts | enquiry
> excess | fortnight | further | grant | hesitate | interest | invoice
> look forward | orders | pleased | receiving | refer | reminder | settlement
> trade | volume | weeks

We *refer*¹ to your ...² of 23 April about our trade and volume ...³.

We ...⁴ a standard ...⁵ discount of 10% on all ...⁶ from commercial ...⁷. In addition, we offer ...⁸ discounts of between 3% and 6% on orders in ...⁹ of €2000, ...¹⁰ on the size of the order.

We are also ...¹¹ to allow a ...¹² of 1.5% for ...¹³ within two ...¹⁴ of receipt of ...¹⁵.

Thank you for your ...¹⁶, and please do not ...¹⁷ to contact me if you have any ...¹⁸ questions.

We ...¹⁹ to ...²⁰ an order from you.

2 Choose the most suitable term.

Thank you for your *enquiry / query / question*¹ of 20 January. We are *glad / happy / pleased*² to submit the following *offer / quotation / tender*³ for fitness machines:

(...)

Please *note / realise / understand*⁴ that all prices include *delivery / despatch / distribution*⁵ to your Bremen *location / property / stores*⁶ at Wiesenstraße 9 by road.

We *affirm / confirm / ensure*⁷ that these prices are 15% below list as an introductory *favour / offer / reward*⁸. We are willing to offer a *discount / rebate / reduction*⁹ of 12.5% on *duplicate / repeat / return*¹⁰ orders up to a *value / total / worth*¹¹ of €5000 and 15% on orders above that *amount / total / volume*¹².

We are also *content / ready / willing*¹³ to allow a cash discount of 2.5% on invoice price for *balance / paying / settlement*¹⁴ within a fortnight of *getting / receiving / receipt*¹⁵ of invoice.

The *goods / material / stuff*¹⁶ will be dispatched *immediately / instantly / simultaneously*¹⁷ on *delivery / presentation / receipt*¹⁸ of order.

We hope that you are *content / gratified / satisfied*¹⁹ with this offer, and we would be delighted to do *business / dealings / trade*²⁰ with you.

3 Complete the phrases with prepositions from the box.

| about | for | in | on | to (3x) | under | with |

1 (to) depend ... sth
2 (to) get ...¹ touch ...² sb
3 (to) phone sb ... sth
4 (to) refer ... sth
5 (to) relate ... sth
6 (to) thank sb ... sth
7 (to) look forward ... doing sth
8 (to) put sb ... pressure

4 Form questions to ask about the underlined part of the statements.

EXAMPLE Barbara works in Brussels now.
Where does Barbara work now?

1 The goods were late because of bad weather in France.
2 I spoke to Janet Brown when I rang the firm.
3 Ajax Computers has placed an order for 500 CD burners.
4 You can place an order by completing an order form.
5 The enquiry was for CD burners.
6 The new delivery is in the stores.
7 I sent Hilary the offer by email.
8 Ben dealt with Ajax's complaint.

Listening comprehension

7 5 You are Pat King. (This name is used for both men and women.) You work in sales at Wessex Fitness Technology Ltd. Listen to the phone call and fill in the key details.

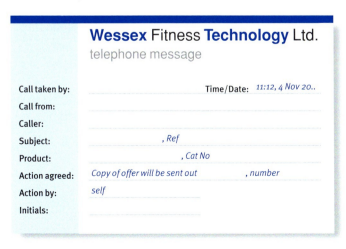

D Writing letters

1 Use the material below to write an offer about camping equipment.

Think up a name and address for your German company and for the British supplier of such products. Add any relevant details such as quantities, models etc.

> **Opening**
> - Thank you for your enquiry about tents/ ... of (Datum).
> - Thank you for your interest in our products.
> - We refer to your enquiry about sleeping bags / ... of (Datum).
>
> **Details**
> - We are happy to send/submit an offer for tents/sleeping bags / ... as follows:
>
> **Terms**
> - All prices include delivery to ...
> - We are pleased/willing to give/offer a trade/volume/introductory discount of ...%.
> - The consignment/goods will be despatched by air/road within ... days on receipt of order.
>
> **Close**
> - Thank you again for your interest in our products.
> - We are certain/sure that you will be (entirely) satisfied with our products.
> - Please do not hesitate to contact / get in touch with us if ...
> - We look forward to receiving an order / doing business with you in due course / the future.

2 Write an offer from notes.

Situation: Sie arbeiten in der Verkaufsabteilung der Firma Dataprint GmbH, einem Hersteller von Computerdruckern. Ihre Anschrift lautet Kirchstr. 23 in 74072 Heilbronn. Die Firma erhält eine Anfrage von Technical Solutions Ltd, 31 Harbour Road, Dublin 7, Ireland. In der Anfrage handelt es sich um die Lieferung von Druckern.

> **Aufgabe**
> Schreiben Sie ein formgerechtes Angebot. Verwenden Sie folgende Angaben:
> - bieten folgende Drucker an: 250 Tintenstrahldrucker (*ink jet printers*) Modell TSD 300 (Listenpreis €210/Stück) und 200 Laserdrucker Modell ND 400 (Listenpreis €175/Stück)
> - 18 % Rabatt auf Gesamtpreis von €87.500 CIF Rotterdam
> - Zahlung durch unwiderrufliches Akkreditiv
> - Lieferung (*dispatch*) innerhalb von 15 Tagen nach Erhalt der Bestellung
> - angemessener Schluss

3 Write a quotation.

Situation: Sie arbeiten für Data-Union GmbH, einen Hersteller von Computer-Peripheriegeräten in 99085 Erfurt, Industriestr. 10.

Aufgabe
Ihr Chef bittet Sie, als Antwort auf unten stehendes Fax ein Angebot für CD-Brenner an Estuary Computers Ltd in Hull zu schicken. Die Einzelheiten sind auf dem Zettel vermerkt.

27/03/20.. 10:47   Fax 49 361 564738   p. 001

ESTUARY Computers Limited
19–21 Humber Road . Hull . HU7 9SY

FAX MESSAGE

To:	Data-Union GmbH	**From:**	Joshua Brown, Purchasing
For:	Beate Taubitz, Export	**Date:**	14 April 20..
Fax no:	+49-361-265748	**Pages**	1
Re:	enquiry		

Dear Ms Taubitz

Thank you for the catalogue and price-lists.

Please quote us for

1 80 (eighty) Superstar CD-burners, order no 5044, list price €215 each
2 60 (sixty) TriSonic CD-burners, order no 7066, list price €375 each

Could you also give us details of your discounts on orders of this size?

Please let us know when we can expect delivery to our Hull plant.

Thank you in advance, and we look forward to receiving your quotation.

Yours sincerely

Joshua Brown

Joshua Brown

Handelsrabatt 15 %, 3 % Skonto bei Zahlung innerhalb von 15 Tagen; zusätzl. Mengenrabatt 5 % bei Aufträgen über € 10.000

Auslieferung per LKW sofort nach Erhalt der Bestellung.

Tel +44-(0)1482 5588-0 ▪ Fax +44-(0)1482 558812 ▪ Email: info@estcom.co.uk
Homepage: www.estcom.co.uk

UNIT 5 Offers and quotations

4 Summarize the letter.

Situation: Sie arbeiten bei der Firma Gustav Wolfson GmbH, einem Großhändler aus der Campingbranche. Sie haben folgendes Angebot über Elektrokühlboxen (*compact fridges*) von einem britischen Hersteller, Camping Technology Ltd, erhalten.

> **Aufgabe**
> Lesen Sie das Angebot und schreiben Sie einen Vermerk in deutscher Sprache für Ihre Chefin, Frau Claudia Holtkamp.

Many thanks for your enquiry of 12 November about our Voyager range of 12V compact fridges.

We are pleased to submit the following firm offer to supply the products you require on the following terms:

1 30 Voyager compact fridges, 26 litre, blue, Order No V26 286   EUR 110 each
2 20 Voyager compact fridges, 45 litre, grey, Order No V45 562   EUR 160 each

As agreed on the telephone and confirmed in our email dated 5 November, these prices are 15% below list. We are also willing to allow a further cash discount of 2.5% on the quoted price provided that payment in full is received within 15 days of receipt of goods.

All prices are CPT your stores at Dieselstraße 27 in 91058 Erlangen, Germany.

(upon firm acceptance of this offer) The consignment will be dispatched immediately by road transport.

This offer is valid for a period of three months from the above date, ie until 18 Feb 20..

In all other cases, our enclosed Terms and Conditions of Business apply.

Many thanks for your interest, and we hope to have the pleasure of meeting your requirements.

---

5 Write an offer from notes.

Situation: Sie sind in der Exportabteilung von MGA-Umwelttechnik GmbH, Nikolaus-Otto-Straße 34, 57075 Siegen, einem Hersteller von Mikrofilteranlagen (*microfiltration plants*), tätig. Die Firma bekommt eine telefonische Anfrage von einer Firma in England.

> **Aufgabe**
> Schreiben Sie ein Angebot an die Firma gemäß folgender Telefonnotizen, die Sie von Ihrem Chef erhalten haben.

- Anruf von Herrn Mark Carter, Cumbrian Power PLC, 12 Glasgow Road, Carlisle CA21 TM4, England
- Interesse an SF 960 Filteranlage für Kohlekraftwerke (*coal-fired power station*)
- telefonisch vereinbart:
  - Rabatt von 17.5 % auf Listenpreis
  - Lieferung CIF Glasgow innerhalb von 4 Wochen nach Auftragsbestätigung
  - Zahlungsbedingung: unwiderrufliches, bestätigtes Akkreditiv
- technisches Datenblatt im beigelegten Prospekt
- über Auftrag würden wir uns sehr freuen; sind sicher, dass die SF 960 alle Anforderungen zu einem äußerst günstigen Preis erfüllen wird (*meet all requirements*)

Offers and quotations UNIT 5 57

E Unit word list

Page 48		offer	*Angebot*
		quotation	*(Preis)Angebot*
		goods	*Güter, Ware*
		services	*Dienstleistungen*
		conditions	*Bedingungen*
		off-the-shelf product	*Standardprodukt*
		terms and conditions of business	*Geschäftsbedingungen*
		in small print	*klein gedruckt*
		special terms	*Sonderbedingungen*
		generous	*großzügig*
		depending on	*je nach*
		finish	*Verarbeitung*
		trade discount	*Handelsrabatt*
		cash discount	*Skonto, Barzahlungsrabatt*
		means of delivery	*Lieferungsmodalitäten*
Page 49		free delivery and transport	*kostenlose Lieferung und Transport*
		below list (price)	*unter Listenpreis*
		within a fortnight of receipt	*innerhalb von 14 Tagen nach Erhalt*
Page 52		in excess of	*über, höher als*
		reminder	*Mahnung*
		settlement (of invoice)	*(Rechnungs)Begleichung*
		tender	*Angebot (für eine Ausschreibung)*
		distribution	*Vertrieb*
		property	*Gebäude, Eigentum*
		stores	*Lager*
		introductory offer	*Einführungsangebot*
		repeat order	*Folgeauftrag*
		total	*Gesamtsumme*
		content	*zufrieden*
Page 53		to depend on	*abhängen von*
		to relate to	*in Verbindung bringen mit*
		to put so. under pressure	*jdn. unter Druck setzen*
		to place an order	*eine Bestellung aufgeben*
Page 54		tent	*Zelt*
		sleeping bag	*Schlafsack*
		entirely	*vollkommen*
Page 55		plant	*Fabrik, Werk*
Page 56		as agreed	*wie vereinbart*
		provided that	*unter der Bedingung, dass*
		upon firm acceptance	*nach verbindlicher Zusage*
		to apply	*gelten*
Useful words		trial order	*Probeauftrag*
		counteroffer	*Gegenangebot*
		to quote a delivery date	*einen Liefertermin nennen*

6 Orders and acknowledgements

Model letters: an order, an acknowledgement

Useful phrases: orders (opening, placing an order, delivery terms); acknowledging an order; cancellation of an order

What are orders and acknowledgements?

When the buyer places an order, he enters into a **contract of sale** with the seller for the delivery of goods and services. The offer (or catalogue plus price-list) and often the seller's **terms and conditions** are the basis for this contract. The order states the exact amounts and types of goods required. It is also common practice for the buyer to repeat the exact **terms of the offer** (discounts, terms of payment and delivery). Today the buyer often only needs to fill in and sign an order form.

The seller only needs to confirm the order, i.e. to write an **acknowledgement of order**, when the terms of the offer have been changed by the buyer.

It may also be necessary to write when the seller cannot supply the goods as offered (goods currently not available or out of stock, delays). In this case, the seller may consider offering a different, but similar, product (**new offer**) and the buyer is expected to agree to the new offer.

How to write orders and acknowledgements of orders

	Orders	Acknowledging the order
Opening	Refer to the offer and say that you wish to place an order.	Thank the customer for the order.
Details	Specify your order (quantity, product number, type, price etc.).	Say when you expect to deliver.
Terms	Confirm the terms and conditions. (Specify a date for delivery.)	
Close	Close with a polite phrase.	Close with a polite phrase.

A Model letters

1 An order

Style Limited
62 Albert Street
London E1 5RT

Tel   +44-(0)20-17 93 77
Fax   +44-(0)20-17 93 88
Email info@styfo.co.uk
Internet www.styfo.co.uk

Textil Dorn GmbH
Karlstraße 10
D-40593 Düsseldorf
Germany

22 December 20..

Order for denim material

Dear Mr Dorn

Thank you for your prompt reply to our enquiry. We would now like to place the following order:

1	10 rolls à 10 m, light stretch denim, blue	LSD 873B	€7.50/m	=	€750.00
2	6 rolls à 10 m, medium stretch denim, black	MSD 728BK	€9.50/m	=	€570.00
3	as 2 above, white	MSD 728W	€9.50/m	=	€570.00

Please note that we have revised the quantities.

We accept the prices and terms as stated in your offer of 18 December. In view of the forthcoming Christmas break, we would ask you to arrange for delivery to be made in the first full week in January.

Thank you for dealing with our enquiry so quickly and we look forward to receiving the goods in due course.

Yours sincerely

Jane Adams
Buyer

Replace parts of the letter above with the following. The answers are not necessarily in the same order.

1. Because of the approaching public holiday
2. replying so quickly
3. for us to receive the goods
4. altered the size of the order
5. You will notice
6. We agree to the terms and conditions of the offer

2 An acknowledgement

Friesenstr. 12   04177 Leipzig   Tel. 03 41/44 53 41
Fax 03 41/44 53 42 34   E-Mail info@tessaconstruct.de
Internet www.tessaconstruct.de

Henderson Engineering Ltd
Unit 23
Ash Industrial Estate
Flex Meadow
Harlow
Essex CM19 5TJ

England

13 October 20..

Contract No. 2756/8

Dear Mr Cox

Please find attached three fully signed copies of the contract for the delivery of warehousing systems which you requested in your fax of 3 October.
You will note that we have included the amendments agreed in our recent exchange of faxes (confirmed and authorised in your fax of 10 October). These changes mainly concern the revised prices and terms of payment.
Please sign next to the changes we have made and return one copy of the contract for our files.
Meanwhile, we are processing your order and it should be ready for dispatch as agreed.
We look forward to hearing from you by return.

Yours sincerely

Angela Palm

Angela Palm

Correct these statements if necessary.

1. The letter is in reply to a message received on 3 October.
2. The copies enclosed need to be signed.
3. The contract has already been negotiated.
4. The contract will be signed on 3 October.
5. No changes have been made.
6. The changes were agreed to in a fax of 10 October.
7. There are probably changes regarding prices and terms.
8. All the changes need to be approved in writing.
9. The recipient should keep one copy.
10. The buyer will be informed when the order is ready for dispatch.

B Useful phrases

1 Orders

Opening

Für die Zusendung Ihres Angebots danken wir.	Thank you for sending us / letting us have your offer.
Für Ihr Angebot vom ... bedanken wir uns. / Ihr Angebot vom ... haben wir dankend erhalten.	Thank you for your offer of ... / We have received your offer of ...
Ihre Muster haben wir sorgfältig getestet/ geprüft.	We have carefully examined/tested your samples/specimens.
Wir finden die Qualität Ihrer Muster zufrieden stellend und Ihre Preise angemessen.	We are pleased with both the quality of your samples and your prices.

Placing an order

Wir beziehen uns auf Ihr Angebot vom ... und möchten nunmehr wie folgt bestellen / folgenden Auftrag erteilen / folgende Bestellung aufgeben:	We refer to / With reference to your offer of ... (and) (we) would like to place the following order:
Nach Ansicht der uns zugeschickten Muster möchten wir wie folgt (zur sofortigen Lieferung) bestellen.	Having looked at the samples/specimens you sent us, we wish to order the following (for immediate delivery).
Unsere Bestellung erfolgt auf der Basis Ihres Katalogs Nr. ...	Our order is based on your catalogue number ...
Anbei finden Sie unsere Bestellung, Nummer 8765, für die nachstehend aufgeführten Artikel: ...	Please find enclosed / We enclose our order, number 8765, for the following items: ...

Delivery terms

Die bestellten Waren müssen sofort geliefert werden.	The goods ordered must be delivered immediately.
Wir müssen darauf bestehen, dass die Waren innerhalb von 10 Tagen geliefert werden.	We must insist that the goods be supplied within ten days.
Wenn Sie innerhalb dieser Zeit/Frist nicht liefern können ...	If you are unable to / If you cannot deliver within this period ...
Die Lieferung erfolgt frei Haus.	Delivery should be franco domicile.
Mit Ihren Liefer- und Zahlungsbedingungen sind wir einverstanden.	We accept your terms of payment and delivery.
Bitte bestätigen Sie den obigen Auftrag sobald wie möglich.	Please confirm the above order as soon as possible.

2 Acknowledging an order

Wir beziehen uns / Unter Bezugnahme auf Ihre Bestellung (Nummer 4848) vom 5. Mai ...	We refer / Referring / With reference to your order (number 4848) of 5 May ...
Wir haben Ihren Auftrag für ... heute erhalten. / Wir bestätigen Ihren Auftrag vom 12. Juli.	We received your order for ... today. / We confirm your order of 12 July.
Wir sind mit Ihrem Vorschlag einverstanden, den Mengenrabatt auf 20 Prozent anzuheben.	We agree to your proposal to increase the volume/quantity discount to 20 per cent.
Bitte haben sie Verständnis dafür, dass wir bei Erstaufträgen auf unseren Zahlungsbedingungen bestehen müssen.	You will understand that we must insist on our terms of payment for initial orders.
Wir sind gern bereit, die Zahlungsbedingungen zu einem späteren Zeitpunkt neu zu verhandeln.	We are, of course, prepared to consider the payment terms again at a later date.
Artikel Nummer 487 ist zur Zeit nicht vorrätig / verfügbar / am Lager.	Item number 487 is not available / not in stock / out of stock at the moment.
Wir benötigen ungefähr zehn Tage, um Ihren Auftrag auszuführen.	We require approximately ten days to complete your order.
Wir werden Ihren Auftrag so bald wie möglich ausführen.	We shall deal with / process your order as soon as possible.

3 Cancellation of an order

Wir möchten unseren Auftrag stornieren.	We wish to cancel our order.
Bitte streichen Sie die folgenden Artikel ...	Please delete the following items ...
Wir behalten uns das Recht vor, den Auftrag zu widerrufen/stornieren / die (Annahme der) Lieferung zu verweigern, wenn ...	We reserve the right to cancel the order / to refuse (to take/accept) delivery if ...
Wir bitten Sie alle Positionen zu stornieren, die nicht bis Monatsende ausgeliefert werden können.	Please cancel all items that cannot be delivered/supplied by the end of the month.

Useful abbreviations

B/E	bill of exchange	Wechsel
B/L	bill of lading	Konnossement, Seefrachtbrief
C/P	carriage paid	frachtfrei, Fracht bezahlt
C/F	carriage forward	Fracht zu Lasten des Empfängers
COD	cash on delivery	Zahlung bei Lieferung, Zahlung per Nachnahme
CWO	cash with order	Barzahlung bei Auftragserteilung
D/A	documents against acceptance	Dokumente gegen Akzept (*Wechsel*)
D/O	delivery order	Auslieferungsschein, Lieferauftrag
D/P	documents against payment	Dokumente gegen Kasse
L/C	letter of credit	Akkreditiv, Kreditbrief
VAT	value added tax	Mehrwertsteuer (MwSt)

Orders and acknowledgements UNIT **6**   63

C Practising language

1 Combine the verbs in group A with the appropriate nouns in group B.

A	B
grant	an order
reserve	delivery
agree	from stock
examine	the requirements
guarantee	the samples
meet	to the terms and conditions
supply	a discount
place	the right

2 Use the most suitable term in the box to replace the expressions in *italics* in the sentences below. There are more terms than you need.

> a fortnight | dispatch | expect delivery to be made | if you do not | is due
> kindly accept | receipt of invoice | order volume | volume | warranty
> we feel that | we reserve the right to | please let us know

1 *In our opinion*, your prices are too high for this market.
2 *Unless you* improve your terms, we will not be able to accept your offer.
3 We are placing this order on condition that you grant us a *quantity* discount of 15 per cent.
4 We *expect to receive the goods* within a week.
5 It is understood that payment *should be made* within two weeks of *the invoice being received*.
6 We will cancel our order if the goods are not delivered within *two weeks*.
7 We understand that your goods are supplied with a six-month *guarantee*.
8 *Kindly inform us* when the goods are ready for *shipment*.

3 Use the following to form meaningful sentences. Add commas where necessary.

1 for your offer / of 2 March / reached us / Thank you / today / which
2 Having examined / meet our requirements / to state that / we are pleased / your goods / your samples
3 for the market / However / in which / are too high / we operate / your prices
4 more favourable discounts / or grant us / to accept / we are unable / Unless you can lower / your offer / your prices
5 are delivered / at the latest / by 15 April / is placed / on condition that / Our order / the goods
6 for your order / our immediate attention / We thank you / which / will have
7 and accept your request / for payment / of 22 February / We acknowledge / within 30 days net / your order
8 and risk / at your cost / Please note that / substandard goods / will be returned

Listening Comprehension

 4 Write a summary in German of the telephone conversation you hear.

Role Play

5 Role-play the following telephone conversation with a partner.

Situation: A ist Mitarbeiter/in im Einkauf bei der Bäumer & Winter GmbH in Balingen bei Stuttgart und hat ein Angebot für Gartenmöbel von **B**, einer/einem Mitarbeiter/in der Henderson Garden Centres in East Grinstead bei London erhalten. **A** ruft **B** an, den/die er kürzlich auf einer Messe kennen gelernt hat, um über die Konditionen zu sprechen.

A	B
introduction, mentions meeting at the trade fair, hopes it was successful for **B**	introduction, asks what he/she can do
	on the whole pleased with the business done
glad to hear that, thanks for prompt reply to enquiry, likes the designs and workmanship of garden furniture displayed at the fair	
	short positive reaction
prices are higher than those of the competitors	
	reacts with surprise and asks for a suggestion
wonders whether prices and terms can be improved	
	thinks that in view of the quality and workmanship prices are fair, asks about possible order volume
replies that in view of the number of outlets (more than 30 garden centres in south and central Germany) the order volume is likely to be very high	
	asks **A** to be more specific
replies that initial order could be in the range of €25,000, further orders to be expected	
	is prepared to grant an additional volume discount of 5 per cent, could be reviewed for follow-up orders
agrees to 5 per cent discount, hopes that more generous discounts will be possible in future	
	thanks for order and will confirm new terms in writing, hopes he will be pleased with the goods, polite end of conversation
polite end of conversation	

Writing letters

1 Use the phrases in the box to write a letter.
Situation: Sie arbeiten in der Einkaufsabteilung einer großen deutschen Gartenartikelkette und haben bei einem britischen Hersteller einige hundert Sonnenschirme mit Ständern (*sunshades with stands*) verschiedener Muster und Farben (*different designs and colour schemes and patterns*) bestellt.

> **Aufgabe**
> Schreiben Sie, dass Sie sich angesichts des verbesserten Angebots zu einer höheren Bestellmenge entschlossen haben. Weisen Sie auf die überarbeitete Bestellung in der Anlage hin und erfinden Sie die passenden Adressen und Einzelheiten.

> **Opening**
> - Thank you for your …
> - We confirm the receipt of your fax/letter of …
> - We are pleased to note / to accept your improved volume discount and payment terms.
> - Thank you for revising your terms.
>
> **Details**
> - As we expect the demand for sunshades to be higher than we originally thought, …
> - We can now offer your sunshades at even more competitive prices.
> - We are confident we will attract even more buyer interest with these lower prices.
>
> **Terms/Solution**
> - We have therefore decided to increase our order / the order volume as follows: …
> - Please find our revised order enclosed.
> - Your revised terms have persuaded us to increase the order volume as listed in the enclosed order form.
> - You will be pleased to learn that we have decided to increase the number of units per item.
>
> **Close**
> - Thank you again for adjusting your terms and we look forward to receiving the goods as agreed.
> - Thank you again for improving your terms and …
> - We would like to confirm that you can still supply the goods by the date originally agreed.
> - Thank you again and we look forward to receiving the goods in due course.

2 Write a reply to this fax message.

Aufgabe

Beantworten Sie diese Fax-Nachricht. Teilen Sie mit, dass Herr Wortmann unmittelbar nach seiner Rückkehr schwer erkrankt ist und deshalb nicht alle Angelegenheiten sofort erledigt wurden. Bitte Sie um Verständnis und Entschuldigung. Sie wollen sich um die Angelegenheit kümmern und werden sich so schnell wie möglich wieder melden. Danken Sie für die Zusendung der Auftragskopie, die Ihnen die Bearbeitung der Angelegenheit (*to deal with the matter*) erleichtert. Bitten Sie nochmals um Verständnis.

Bushmill Engineering LTD

11-15 O'Leary Street
Limerick Ireland
Tel 061 43679-0
Fax 061 43679-234
www.Bushmillengineering.com.ie
Email info@bushmillengineering.com.ie

FAX MESSAGE

Date: 15 February 20..
To: Winter Maschinenbau GmbH Pforzheim   Fax 07231/46 47 3811
For: Herr Wortmann
Pages: 1

About: **Order confirmation**

Dear Mr Wortmann

During your visit to us in January, we placed a major order with you for the supply of metal working machines. At the time you promised to send us the relevant documentation immediately after your return to Germany. Unfortunately, we are still awaiting your confirmation of this order. We need the machines as soon as possible and would like you to confirm our order. Could you also inform us whether you would prefer payment by L/C or cash against documents? We have attached a copy of our order for your reference. We hope to hear from you very soon.
Yours sincerely

Ken McDougal

Ken McDougal
(Production Manager)

3 Write an email as a reply to an offer.

Situation: Lesen Sie das Fax auf S. 55 noch einmal. Joshua ist nicht sehr glücklich über die hier genannten Preise und versucht, bei den Preisen und Bedingungen nachzuverhandeln.

> **Aufgabe**
> Danken Sie für das Fax vom 14 April. Drücken Sie Ihre Enttäuschung über die Preise und sonstigen Bedingungen aus. Die Preise liegen über den Einzelhandelspreisen (*retail prices*) in Großbritannien. Bitten Sie darum, die Preise und Rabatte noch einmal zu überdenken, da sonst ein Geschäft nicht zustande kommen kann. Geben Sie zu bedenken, dass die Preise sich in dieser Branche rasch verändern und generell nach unten tendieren. Erbitten Sie eine rasche Antwort.

4 Write a letter from notes.

Situation: Als Mitarbeiter/in der Einkaufsabteilung der Wassermann Elektronik GmbH & Co KG, Döbbrick-Süd 98, 03054 Cottbus bearbeiten Sie die Auslandsbestellungen. Schreiben Sie ein Fax.

> **Aufgabe**
> Beziehen Sie sich auf das Angebot der Samsung IT Engineering Ltd, Dainong Mapo Building, 47-4 Myonmok-dong, Pusan 621-423, South Korea für die Lieferung von Elektronik-Zubehörteilen (*electronic parts*).
> - Auftragserteilung gemäß beigefügtem Auftragsformular
> - Wegen des Auftragsvolumens Bitte um höheren Mengenrabatt
> - Lieferung gemäß Angebot spätestens 8 Wochen nach Auftragserteilung CIF Hamburg
> - Zahlung per L/C, deshalb bitte umgehende Zusendung einer Pro-forma-Rechnung (*pro forma invoice*)
> - Bitte um Auftragsbestätigung
> - Bei zufrieden stellender Erledigung sind Folgeaufträge möglich

Unit word list

Page 58	acknowledgement/confirmation of (an) order	Auftragsbestätigung
	terms of the offer	Angebotsbedingungen
	terms of payment	Zahlungsbedingungen
	delivery terms, terms of delivery	Lieferbedingungen
	order form	Auftragsformular
	to be out of stock	nicht (mehr) vorrätig sein
	to specify	genaue Angaben machen zu
Page 59	to revise	verändern
	to note	zur Kenntnis nehmen
	forthcoming	bevorstehend
	to arrange for delivery to be made	Lieferung veranlassen
	in due course	bald, zu gegebener Zeit
Page 60	amendment (*Vertrag*)	Ergänzung
	to authorise	genehmigen, zustimmen zu
	revised terms	verbesserte Bedingungen/ Konditionen
	for our files	für unsere Unterlagen
	meanwhile	zwischenzeitlich
	to process an order	Auftrag ausführen
	ready for dispatch/shipment	versandfertig, versandbereit
	to negotiate	verhandeln
Page 63	warranty, guarantee	Gewährleistung, Garantie
	to cancel an order	Auftrag stornieren
	to meet s.o.'s requirements	jds. Bedürfnissen entsprechen
	will have our immediate attention	wird umgehend bearbeitet
	request	Bitte
	substandard	minderwertig
Page 64	workmanship	Verarbeitung
	furniture	Möbel
	in view of	angesichts
	to be likely to	wird wahrscheinlich
	specific	hier: *genau*
	follow-up order	Folgeauftrag
Page 65	competitive prices	wettbewerbsfähige Preise
	to adjust	korrigieren, anpassen
Page 66	major	groß, größer
	to attach	beilegen
Useful words	adequate stock levels	ausreichender (Waren)Bestand
	advantageous	günstig, vorteilhaft
	competitive situation	Wettbewerbslage
	contract of sale	Kaufvertrag
	for display purposes	für Ausstellungszwecke
	home/domestic market	heimischer Markt; Binnenmarkt
	outlet	Verkaufsstelle
	top-quality	hochwertig, von erstklassiger Qualität

7 Dealing with orders

Model letters: asking for the reasons of a delay in delivery, reply stating reasons for delay, transport arrangements

Useful phrases: dealing with orders; supplier's delivery periods; buyer's request for delivery; transport arrangements

What happens when an order has been placed?

Once the order has been received and accepted, the supplier will get the goods **ready for dispatch**.

When goods are supplied from stock, delivery can be made immediately. If, however, the goods are made to the customer's specifications (**customised goods**), production may take longer. If the seller fails to deliver the goods on time, the customer usually sends an enquiry about the delay. Delays are especially serious with goods shipped abroad because complex matters of transportation (packing, means of transport, sharing of costs and risks, time schedules) need to be clarified (cf. **INCO-Terms**).

How to deal with order processing issues

	Enquiry about a delay in delivery	Replying to an enquiry about a delay in delivery	Dispatch. Shipping arrangements
Opening	Refer to the order and promised delivery date.	Refer to the enquiry about the delivery date.	Refer to the order.
Details	Express your surprise at the delay.	Apologise for the delay and state reason(s).	State that the goods are ready for shipment.
Action	State why you need the goods urgently. Indicate consequences of further delay.	State what you are going to do to speed up the delivery.	Give all the relevant details about the delivery.
Close	Express hope for speedy delivery. Close with a polite phrase.	(Apologise again.) Ask for understanding. Close with a polite phrase.	Express hope that goods will arrive safely. Close with a polite phrase.

UNIT 7 Dealing with orders

A Model letters

1 Asking for the reasons for a delay in delivery

Leith Weaving Ltd
12 Palmerston Road
Tel 0131-45672-1
Email: Ann.Spears@leithweaving.co.uk
Internet: www.leithweaving.co.uk

Forth Industrial Park
Leith EH15 4TG
Fax 0131-45672-240

Langley Engineering Solutions (LES) Ltd
Cambridge Science Park
Milton Road
Cambridge
CB4 0GW

20 August 20..

Order for tartan fabrics

Dear Ms Soames

We are surprised that our goods (order no. 1186/27) have not arrived yet. In your letter of 11 July, you promised shipment by the beginning of August and we advised our customers accordingly.

We quite understand that delays are sometimes unforeseen and unavoidable. However, it is usual to at least inform the customer and we are rather disappointed that we did not hear from you about any problems.

We look forward to your reply.

Yours sincerely

Ann Spears
(Buyer)

2 Reply stating reasons for delay

> 24 August 20..
>
> Your order No. 1186/27
>
> Dear Ms Spears
>
> We acknowledge the receipt of your letter of 20 August and must apologise for the delay in the execution of your order. The last delivery of the tartan materials from the factory was slightly off-shade but, as we were expecting new supplies within a matter of days, we thought we did not need to write to you. We are sorry that you have been inconvenienced but want to assure you that your order has had our usual, careful attention.
> A new consignment has arrived today so we can now begin manufacturing your goods and expect to deliver your order within the next few days.
> We apologise once again for the delay and hope it has not caused you any serious trouble.
>
> Yours sincerely
>
> Judy Soames
> (Sales Officer)

a Correct these statements about the letters.

1 Order no. 1286/37 is for tartan fabrics.
2 The order was due to be delivered by 20 August.
3 The buyer didn't advise his customers of the delivery date.
4 Delays are always unavoidable.
5 The customer was informed of the delay.
6 New fabric arrived on 22 August.
7 Ms Spears signs the letter dated 24 August.
8 The tartan materials were of a different colour from that ordered.

b Complete these phrases with the appropriate verbs from the letters.

1 to ... shipment
2 to ... a customer
3 to ... from somebody
4 to ... the receipt of a letter
5 to ... for a delay
6 to ... manufacturing
7 to ... an order
8 to ... serious trouble

3 Transport arrangements

Stolte & Hagen

Stolte & Hagen GmbH   Oderstr. 64   01109 Dresden
Tel 0351-34 12 1-0   Fax 0351-34 12 1-211   E-Mail Info@stolte-hagen.de   www.stolte-hagen.de

Hartleby & Baines Ltd
245 Oldham Road
Halifax
HX12 4PZ

England

24 April 20..

Your order for plastic seats

Dear Mr Darling

Thank you again for your order of 21 March for plastic seats. The order is nearly complete and we expect to make delivery early next week.
The goods have been carefully packed and palletised for easy handling as agreed. As requested, we have arranged for the transport to be carried out by Spedition Sundermann, a local haulier. They will contact you about further details and also issue a separate invoice for their transport services.
Please find our invoice enclosed. As per our contract, we expect settlement within a fortnight of receipt of the goods. We hope the consignment reaches you in good condition and thank you again for your order.

Yours sincerely

U. Hinrichs

U. Hinrichs
(Versandabteilung)

Here are some statements about the letter above. Ask questions about the parts in *italics* using the question words in brackets.

1 The order is *for plastic seats*. (what?)
2 Delivery can be made *early next week*. (when?)
3 The goods are palletised *for easy handling*. (why?)
4 *Spedition Sundermann, a local haulier*, will be responsible for transport. (who?)
5 The hauliers *will contact* Hartleby & Baines Ltd. (what?)
6 They will issue *a separate invoice for transport services*. (what?)
7 The invoice for the goods is *enclosed*. (where?)
8 They expect settlement of the invoice *within a fortnight of receipt of the goods*. (when?)

B Useful phrases

1 Dealing with orders

Wir haben Ihren Auftrag für … heute erhalten. / Wir danken für / bestätigen Ihren Auftrag vom 12. Juli.	We received your order for … today. / Thank you for / We confirm your order of 12 July.
Artikel Nummer 487 ist zur Zeit nicht vorrätig / verfügbar / am Lager.	Item number 487 is not available / not in stock / is out of stock at the moment.
Deshalb können wir die Lieferung bis zum 4. März nicht garantieren.	Therefore, we cannot guarantee delivery by 4 March.
Wir benötigen ungefähr zehn Tage, um Ihren Auftrag auszuführen.	We require approximately ten days to complete your order.
Wir können erst im August mit der Herstellung beginnen.	We cannot start manufacture until August.

2 Supplier's delivery periods

Wir bestätigen den Liefertermin, den Sie in Ihrem Brief angegeben haben.	We confirm the delivery date you stipulated / requested / asked for in your letter.
Wir können die Waren früher als vereinbart / sofort / bis spätestens 10. August liefern.	We can deliver the goods earlier than agreed / immediately / by 10 August at the latest.
Unsere kürzeste Lieferzeit beträgt einen Monat.	Our earliest delivery time would be in one month's time.
Wir werden die Waren bis Anfang Mai versandbereit haben.	We shall have the goods ready for shipment by the beginning of May.
Die von Ihnen bestellten Waren sind abholbereit/versandbereit.	The goods you ordered await collection / are ready for collection / are ready for dispatch/shipment.
Die Lieferungsverzögerung ist auf … zurückzuführen.	The delay in delivery is due to …
Es wird nicht möglich sein, die Waren innerhalb der vereinbarten Frist von 2 Monaten zu liefern.	It will not be possible to deliver the goods within the agreed period of 2 months.
Wir haben mit der Herstellung der Waren begonnen.	We have started the manufacture of your goods.
Die Lieferung erfolgt innerhalb von 4 Monaten.	Delivery will take place within 4 months.

3 Buyer's request for delivery

Bitte teilen Sie uns mit, wann die Lieferung erfolgen wird.	Please let us know when delivery will be made.
Dieser Auftrag ist dringend, und wir wären Ihnen dankbar, wenn Sie den sofortigen Versand / die sofortige Auslieferung veranlassen könnten.	This order is urgent and we would appreciate it if you could arrange for immediate shipment/delivery.
Die Lieferungsverzögerung hat uns erhebliche Schwierigkeiten bereitet.	The delay in delivery has caused us considerable problems.
Die Waren müssen bis Ende nächsten Monats geliefert werden.	The goods must be delivered by the end of next month.
Die Lieferung muss rechtzeitig erfolgen.	Delivery must be made on time.
Wir können die Ware nicht annehmen, wenn sie nicht rechtzeitig geliefert wird.	We cannot accept the goods if they are not delivered on time.
Wir haben die Waren/Sendung noch nicht erhalten.	We have not yet received the goods.
Die Sendung, die Sie für den 13. Februar zugesagt hatten, ist bisher noch nicht eingetroffen.	The consignment you promised to deliver on 13 February has not arrived yet.

4 Transport arrangements

In Ihrem Auftrag wird nicht angegeben, wie die Waren transportiert werden sollen.	Your order does not state/say/mention how the goods should be transported.
Die Kisten sind vom Spediteur abgeholt worden.	The cases have been collected by the carriers.
Wir werden alle Güter in einer einzelnen Sendung schicken.	We shall send all the goods in a single consignment.
Die Sendung besteht aus zwei Kisten zu je 50 Kilo.	The consignment consists of two cases, each weighing 50 kilos.
Die Waren wurden heute / am 9. Juni an Sie versandt.	The goods were dispatched / sent to you today / on 9 June.
Das Schiff soll am 21. Juli in Felixstowe eintreffen.	The ship should arrive in Felixstowe on 21 July.

per / mit der Bahn	by rail
mit dem Flugzeug / auf dem Luftwege; als/per Luftfracht	by air; as/by air freight
mit dem Schiff / auf dem Seeweg	by ship
mit LKW/Lastkraftwagen	by lorry/truck; by road
Fracht bezahlt/frachtfrei	carriage/freight paid
Fracht zu Lasten des Empfängers	carriage/freight forward
ausschließlich/einschließlich Fracht	exclusive/inclusive of freight/carriage

C Practising language

1 Complete this letter using the words in the box. There are more items than you need.

> apologise for | are pleased | At this stage | be fair to | deal with orders
> delay in delivery | due to | everything we can | keep you informed | order for
> process your order | unfortunately | we are sorry | you will realise

Dear Mr Williams

Thank you for your ... ¹ laminated security glass of 5 July which we ... ² to confirm. However, ... ³ to have to inform you that, ... ⁴ the breakdown of one of our machines, there will be a ... ⁵ of at least a week. We are doing ... ⁶ to have the machine repaired as soon as possible. But ... ⁷ that parts have to be flown in and fitted. To ... ⁸ all our customers, we have decided to ... ⁹ on a strict rota basis. We will ... ¹⁰ about the progress of the repair work here. ... ¹¹ we would like to thank you for your understanding and ... ¹² the inconvenience caused.

Yours sincerely

2 Saying you are sorry.

Use verbs or verbal expressions from the table to fill the gaps. You may have to change the structure of the following verb as well. Sometimes more than one answer is possible.

formal	informal/spoken
to apologise for | to excuse	to regret | to be sorry
to offer one's apologies (for)	

EXAMPLE: I ... for being more than half an hour late.
I'm sorry for being more than half an hour late.

1 We ... not to be able to deliver the machine by the date agreed in our contract.
2 We ... for this delay. But it was not our fault.
3 I ... to give you the wrong information.
4 I misread the order number. Please ... me.
5 I ... not to have told you about this earlier.
6 We realise that this late delivery has made trading difficult for you and ...
7 Please ... the late arrival of this consignment, which is entirely due to reasons beyond our control.
8 We ... to have caused you this inconvenience.

3 Decide which is the correct term. If in doubt, consult your dictionary.

1 We acknowledge the delivery date you *commanded / demanded / stipulated* in your order.
2 The goods can be supplied earlier than *agreed / set up / contracted*.
3 The earliest *consignment / delivery / supply* date is two weeks from the date of your order.
4 We promise to start production upon *receipt / reception / recipe* of your order.
5 Please let us have your *commands / instructions / orders* for shipment as soon as possible.
6 Our delivery dates must be strictly *adhered to / obeyed / watched*.
7 Our forwarding agent will *contact you / contract you / inform you* regarding the details of the transport arrangements.
8 We are pleased to confirm that, in accordance with your *shipping / supply / ship* instructions, we have handed over your consignment to our forwarding agent today.

4 Describe the chart.

Situation: Sie sind Mitarbeiter/in der Versandabteilung der deutschen Tochtergesellschaft eines international tätigen Konzerns mit Sitz in den USA. Für eine Tagung der Versandleiter bereiten Sie Statistiken über die Entwicklung der Auftragsbearbeitungszeiten (Zeit zwischen Auftragseingang und Auslieferung) vor.

> **Aufgabe**
> Erstellen Sie einen englischsprachigen Text und beschreiben Sie die Entwicklung in dem fraglichen Zeitraum.

Auftragsbearbeitungszeiten*

	Standort			
Jahr	Böblingen	Chemnitz	Kiel	Nordhausen
2000	6,37	5,8	6,08	6,85
2001	6,01	5,35	5,71	6,68
2002	5,89	5,71	5,42	6,31
2003	6,21	5,27	5,33	5,84
2004	5,76	5,04	5,15	5,36

*in Arbeitstagen

5 Summarize the letter.

Situation: Sie arbeiten in der Einkaufsabteilung eines Maschinenbauunternehmens in Eschweiler. Die Lieferung der bestellten Schneidemaschinen soll vereinbarungsgemäß in den nächsten Tagen erfolgen.

> **Aufgabe**
> Fassen Sie für den Abteilungsleiter den Inhalt dieses Schreibens in Deutsch zusammen. Berücksichtigen Sie dabei besonders die Informationen zu Verpackung, Transport and Ankunft der Waren.

Dear Mr Neubert

Thank you for your order no. 5643 B/D of 28 May. We are pleased to inform you that the manufacture of your cutting machines is nearing completion.

As requested, we will ship the machines by air. The goods have been packed in 5 wooden crates measuring 1.2 x 2.2 x 0.75m which are lined with water-proof padding material to avoid damage from shock and moisture. The cases carry the customary caution marks.
The goods will be collected from our premises by FT Express Services and put on one of their planes. The scheduled arrival at Liège airport is 12.30 hrs on Wednesday 26 June. As per our agreement, you will arrange for forward carriage to your works in Eschweiler.

We hope that the consignment arrives punctually and in good condition and we look forward to further orders.

Yours sincerely

Chris Hutton
(Despatch Manager)

Listening Comprehension

6 Listen to the first telephone conversation about a delivery problem and answer questions 1–5. Then listen to the second conversation and answer questions 6–10.

Mr. Cunningham wants to discuss a delivery problem with Ms Kourgialis.
1 Which company does Mr Cunningham work for?
2 Where has Ms Kourgialis gone?
3 Will Ms Kourgialis be back later in the day?
4 What message did the secretary take?
5 Does Ms Kourgialis have Mr Cunningham's number?

Ms Kourgialis phones Mr Cunningham the next morning.
6 Why wasn't Ms Kourgialis in the office on the day before?
7 What was the promised delivery date?
8 When will the goods be delivered?
9 What is the problem Mr Cunningham talks about?
10 What is the solution Mr Cunningham suggests?

Now take the part of Mr Cunningham and write a short memo for your principal.

D Writing letters

1 Use suitable sentences from the list below to inform your customer about a delay in delivery.

Situation: Wegen einer unerwarteten Auftragsflut (*rush of orders*) in den letzten 10 Tagen sind die Farbe und das Material eines vom Kunden bestellten Produkts nicht mehr am Lager. Die anderen Materialien und Farben aus dem Auftrag sind allerdings sofort lieferbar. Neue Ware wird innerhalb von 14 Tagen erwartet.

> **Aufgabe**
> Bitten Sie den Kunden um Anweisungen (*instructions*), ob andere Materialien/Farben geschickt werden sollen oder ob die Bearbeitung des Auftrags zurückgestellt werden soll, bis die neue Ware eingetroffen ist.

Opening
- Thank you (very much) for your order of …
- We are pleased to acknowledge receipt of your letter of …
- We have received your letter of and …

Details
- (You will be pleased to learn that) All the items are in stock / are ready for dispatch / can be shipped except for …
- (However,) we are sorry to have to inform you …
- We are sorry to say that …
- Due to an unexpectedly high demand, the following items are (temporarily) out of stock.
- Unfortunately, we are unable to supply these goods at present / at the moment.

Action
- We expect new supplies within a week/fortnight at the latest.
- As new supplies are expected within a few days / a fortnight, we would suggest that we hold your order until then.
- Of course, we could send/dispatch the available goods immediately and ship the remainder (free of charge) as soon as the new supplies have come in.

Close
- We hope to hear from you soon.
- Please let us know what you want us to do.
- We apologise once again for the inconvenience and look forward to receiving your instructions by return.
- Thank you for your understanding and we promise to dispatch your goods as soon as possible.

2 Write a letter/fax informing a customer about a delay in delivery for this order.

> **Aufgabe**
> Schreiben Sie unter Bezugnahme auf den Auftrag eine Fax-Nachricht. Teilen Sie der Derby Warehousing Ltd mit, dass sich die Auslieferung des Regalmaterials um ca. 2 Wochen verzögern wird, weil auf Grund von Lieferproblemen bei Unterlieferanten (*sub-suppliers*) wichtige Vormaterialien (*input materials*) leider nicht rechtzeitig zur Verfügung standen. Beim derzeitigen Stand der Produktion kann mit dem Beginn der Montage Anfang Juni gerechnet werden. Bitten Sie um Entschuldigung und Verständnis. Ein Teil der Zeit wurde durch Produktionsumstellung aufgeholt. Die genaue Terminplanung wird in den nächsten Tagen erstellt und umgehend zugesandt.

Derby Warehousing Ltd

12-14 Leicester Street
Derby DE5 9BN
Tel 01332-75764-1
Fax 01332-75764-500
Email info@derby-warehouse.co.uk
www.derby-warehouse.co.uk

Melchers & Schmitt GmbH & Co KG
Fabrikzeile
95028 Hof
Germany

Order for shelving system Orion

Dear Mr Schumacher

We refer to your offer of 25 March and our telephone conversation of 1 April. We would like to place an order for the equipment of our entire warehouse with the Orion shelving system on the basis of your offer and the subsequent changes in prices and discount. Please find the full details in our supply contract, two copies of which are enclosed.

We would like to confirm the main points of this contract. It is agreed that the price of £275,000 covers the delivery and assembly of the shelving system at our premises. The amount is payable in three instalments: £75,000 within a week of your acceptance of our order, £100,000 upon delivery of the equipment at our premises and the remainder after the full and satisfactory completion of the assembly.

The shelving system will be delivered in the second week of May and you will start assembly work within 5 days of delivery at the very latest. The assembly is scheduled to take a full working week. Penalty clauses apply in case of a delay in the assembly work.

Please sign the contract and return one copy to us.

We look forward to hearing from you in the near future.

Yours sincerely

Peter Fisher
Managing Director

3 Write an email from notes.

Situation: Mit Ihrem Lieferanten (Joe Mackintosh Ltd, 287 Falkirk Road, Stirling FK25 3GD) hatte Ihre Firma (Woll-Import & Handelsgesellschaft mbH, Hansakai 56, 27472 Cuxhaven) die Lieferung von größeren Mengen von Wollstoffen verschiedener Art vereinbart. Der geplante Liefertermin ist um mehr als eine Woche überschritten.

> **Aufgabe**
> Verfassen Sie eine E-Mail an Joe Macintosh Ltd. unter Berücksichtigung folgender Punkte:
> - Bezug auf Auftrag und vereinbarte Termine
> - Grund für den Lieferverzug?
> - Produktion gefährdet
> - Bitte um umgehende Mitteilung des Liefertermins
> - Hinweis auf mögliche Konsequenzen (keine Folgeaufträge)
> - angemessener Briefschluss

4 Write a letter from notes.

Situation: Die Firma Airdale Manufacturing Ltd., 46-48 Belfast Road, Dublin, Irland, hatte bei Ihnen (Mettler Maschinenbau GmbH, Sommerstr. 47, 90762 Fürth) Maschinenteile bestellt. Die Produktion ist nahezu abgeschlossen. Erstellen Sie eine Versandanzeige.

> **Aufgabe**
> Teilen Sie dem Kunden mit, dass die Artikel aus dem Auftrag GBZ 8971 in den nächsten Tagen zum Versand gebracht werden. Gehen Sie dabei auf folgende Punkte ein:
> - Bezugnahme auf Auftrag
> - Mitteilung über Stand der Produktion
> - Auslieferung in der 24. Kalenderwoche
> - Transport erfolgt durch Hansa-Transport GmbH
> - Gemäß Auftrag erfolgt Zahlung bei Lieferung – Bitte um Rücksendung der beigefügten Tratte nach Annahme (*draft for acceptance*)
> - Dank für Auftrag und Hoffnung auf Zufriedenheit mit der Auftragsausführung
> - Angemessene Schlussformel

E Unit word list

Page 69	delivery period	*Lieferfrist*
	transport arrangements	*Transportvereinbarungen*
	to make to customer's specifications	*nach Kundenangaben herstellen/ anfertigen*
	customised	*nach Kundenangaben hergestellt/ gefertigt*
	to ship	*versenden, verfrachten, verschiffen*
	packing, packaging	*Verpackung*
	means of transport	*Transportmittel*
	clarify	*klären*
	delay in delivery	*Lieferverzug; Verzögerung in der (Aus)Lieferung*
	delivery date	*Liefertermin*
Page 70	shipment	*Sendung, Ladung, Lieferung, Partie*
	to advise	*informieren, in Kenntnis setzen*
Page 71	to inconvenience s.o.	*jdm. Unannehmlichkeiten bereiten*
Page 72	to make delivery	*(aus)liefern*
	to palletise	*auf Paletten verpacken*
	handling	*Handhabung, Transport*
	(road) haulier, haulage company	*(Straßen)Spediteur, (Güter)Spedition*
	as per	*gemäß*
Page 75	on a strict rota basis, in strict rotation	*genau der Reihe nach*
	late delivery	*verspätete Lieferung*
Page 76	instructions for shipment/dispatch; shipping instructions	*Versandanweisungen*
	to strictly adhere to	*genau einhalten*
	forwarding/shipping agent	*Spediteur, Spedition*
Page 77	to line *(Kiste)*	*ausschlagen*
	padding material	*Füllmaterial*
	caution marks	*Markierungen*
	forward carriage / on-carriage	*Weitertransport*
	principal	*Mandant/in, Klient/in*
Page 78	except for	*außer*
	demand	*Nachfrage*
	temporarily	*zeitweilig*
	remainder	*Rest*
	free of charge	*kostenlos*
Page 79	supply contract	*Liefervertrag*
	it is agreed	*es gilt als vereinbart*
Useful words	advice of dispatch/shipment, advice note	*Versandanzeige*
	delivery commitments	*Lieferverpflichtungen*
	delivery/dispatch note	*Lieferschein*
	to ensure	*sicher stellen, gewährleisten*
	freight forwarder	*Spedition, Spediteur*
	shipper	*Versender, Absender; Spedition(sfirma)*

8 Payments and reminders

Model letters: letter requesting payment, first reminder, second and final reminder, reply to a first or second reminder

Useful phrases: sending an invoice / a statement and asking for payment; reminder; delayed payment terms; making and confirming payment

How is payment obtained?

The seller usually sends the invoice when the goods have been delivered. The invoice includes the details of the transaction, the time allowed for payment and also the cash discount. If there are problems with the invoice (accounting errors, wrong goods etc.), the buyer will point out any **discrepancies** and can expect the mistake to be put right.

If payment is not made on time, the seller sends a friendly **request for payment**, often a standard letter combined with the offer of new goods. The **first reminder (collection letter)** is normally accompanied by a copy of the invoice and states a final date for payment. The second reminder is friendly but insistent in tone and gives the buyer a final **deadline for payment**. All the relevant details are stated and the possibility of legal action is mentioned.

How to deal with order processing issues

	Request for payment	First/second reminder	Reply to reminders
Opening	Refer to the transaction.	Refer to the transaction and state disappointment at not having received payment.	Refer to the transaction and apologise for delay.
Details	State that payment may have been overlooked.	Repeat payment terms. Remind the customer of duty to pay for goods/services.	State why payment was withheld.
Action	Ask for payment to be made.	Ask for payment to be made immediately and state period/date.	State that you are paying now or ask for extension. (Apologise again.)
Close	Close with a polite phrase.	Express hope for speedy settlement. Close with a polite phrase.	Thank the supplier for understanding. Close with a polite phrase.

A Model letters

1 Letter requesting payment

20 June 20..

Our invoice No. 5421/05

Dear Ms Dixon

We refer to our consignment of video tapes and the attached invoice No. 5421/05. According to our records we have not yet had any payment from you. We are sure our invoice has been simply overlooked. Please ensure that your remittance is made without delay.
Thank you for your attention.

Yours sincerely

Sylvia Fuchs

Sylvia Fuchs

2 First reminder

20 July 20..

Our invoice No. 5421/05

Dear Ms Dixon

This is to inform you that, according to our records, we have not yet received the amount of £2,004.50 due from our invoice No. 5421/05. The amount is now more than eight weeks overdue. We would like to remind you that payment was due within a fortnight from the date of invoice and we kindly ask you to clear your account without further delay. If you have transferred the outstanding sum in the meantime, please disregard this letter.
We would appreciate it if you could send payment as soon as possible.
We look forward to receiving your remittance by return.

Yours sincerely

Sylvia Fuchs

Sylvia Fuchs

3 Second and final reminder

> 20 August 20..
>
> Our invoice No. 5421/05
>
> Dear Ms Dixon
>
> We are disappointed that we have to write to you again about the settlement of our invoice No. 5421/05. You will realise that the amount of £2,004.50 is now twelve weeks overdue. We fail to understand why we have received neither payment nor an explanation for your delay in clearing your account. We enclose a copy of our invoice for your information and must ask you to give this matter your immediate attention. Unless we receive your transfer within the next ten days or a satisfactory explanation for your delay in payment, we will have no choice but to turn the matter over to our solicitor. It is up to you now to help us to avoid such a step.
> We hope to receive your remittance by return.
>
> Yours sincerely
>
> *Sylvia Fuchs*
>
> Sylvia Fuchs

a Complete these sentences.

1 Two weeks ago we sent you a ... of video tapes.
2 Our records show that ... No. 5421/05 is still outstanding.
3 Please let us have your ... promptly.
4 Payment is now more than eight weeks ...
5 The letter can be ... if payment of the ... amount has been made in the meantime.
6 Ms Fuchs would ... it if the customer paid the outstanding amount as soon as ...
7 Ms Fuchs is looking forward to the account being settled ...
8 Ms Fuchs writes to the customer a third time to ask for the ... of invoice No. 5421/05.
9 Ms Dixon is asked to give the matter her ...
10 If payment is not made immediately, a ... will be asked to deal with the matter.

b Let's establish the facts.

1 What kind of product did the customer buy?
2 Can you remember the invoice number?
3 What is the invoice amount?
4 Work out when the invoice was due for payment.
5 What were the terms of payment?
6 How much time has passed between the date of invoice and the first reminder?
7 How much time has passed when the final reminder is sent?
8 What is the deadline for payment when the final reminder arrives?

4 Reply to a first or second reminder

baumann webwise
Die IT-Profis

Intelligent PC Supplies Inc
5736 14th Street NE
St. Paul
Minnesota MN 55232
U.S.A.

31 August 20..

Your request for payment

Dear Mr Cunningham:

We refer to our order No. 2048X7 and your invoice G 4758 of 21 May and apologise most sincerely for the delay in clearing our account. Your reminders did not go unnoticed and it is certainly not our practice to exceed our credit periods.

It is due to events beyond our control that we delayed settling your account. Unfortunately, two of our best customers have recently gone out of business which made it difficult for us to meet all our financial obligations promptly, especially considering the current problematic business climate.

We are pleased to state, however, that our efforts to stabilise our cash flow are now beginning to pay off. Therefore, we have paid $10,000.00 today and will transfer the remainder of $10,345.00 in a month's time. We hope you will understand our situation and appreciate that we are making every effort to clear our account as soon as we can.

Thank you in advance for your understanding and patience.

Sincerely yours,

Annika Tauber
(Accounts Dept)

baumann webwise GmbH
Naumburger Str. 27
04229 Leipzig
Tel   0341-879571-1
Fax 0341-879571-223
E-Mail info@webwise-leipzig.de
www.webwise-leipzig.de

Decide which parts of the letter above can be replaced by the following expressions. They are in the same order.

a Referring to
b offer our sincere apologies
c in settling your invoice
d requests for payment
e we do not normally
f payment
g bankrupt

h commitments
i difficult business situation
j our attempts
k outstanding amount
l are doing all we can
m as quickly
n Yours truly

B Useful phrases

1 Sending an invoice / a statement and asking for payment

Als Anlage senden wir Ihnen / Anbei finden Sie unsere Rechnung Nr. ... für die am 3. Mai gelieferten Waren.	Please find enclosed / We enclose our invoice no. ... for the goods delivered to you on 3 May.
Wir bitten um baldige/umgehende Begleichung unserer Rechnung.	We kindly ask for early settlement of / ask you to settle our invoice by return.
Die Zahlung der Rechnung erbitten wir auf das Konto Nr. ...	We request payment of our invoice to account number ...
Wir legen unseren Auszug für das 2. Quartal bei.	We enclose our statement for the second quarter.
Der (zu zahlende) Gesamtbetrag beläuft sich auf ...	The total amount payable is ...
Wir haben den üblichen Rabatt von ... % schon von Ihrer Rechnung abgezogen.	We have already deducted the customary discount of ...% from your invoice.

2 Reminder

Unsere Rechnung Nr. ... ist noch offen.	Our invoice no. ... is still unpaid.
Da der fällige Betrag schon seit langer Zeit / seit vier Wochen offen steht / überfällig ist, ...	As the unpaid/outstanding amount is considerably / four weeks overdue, ...
Ihr Konto weist noch einen Minusbetrag von ... auf.	Your account still shows a debit balance of ....
Bitte senden Sie uns den fälligen Betrag in den nächsten Tagen.	Please let us have the amount due within the next few days.
Wir erwarten Ihre Zahlung/Überweisung bis spätestens zum ...	We await your payment/remittance/ transfer by ... at the latest.
Wir möchten Sie daran erinnern, dass unsere Zahlungsbedingungen ... sind.	We wish to remind you that our terms of payment are ...
Bis jetzt haben wir auf unsere Bitte um Zahlung keine Antwort erhalten.	We have as yet had no reply to our request for payment.
Trotz unserer wiederholten Zahlungs- aufforderungen ...	Despite our repeated requests for payment ...
Wir müssen Sie daran erinnern, dass wir bei Erstaufträgen nur zwei Wochen Ziel gewähren.	We must remind you that we only allow two weeks credit for first orders.
Dies ist unsere letzte Mahnung.	This is our last/final request for payment.
Wir müssen jetzt auf sofortiger Zahlung / Begleichung unserer Rechnung bestehen.	We must now insist on immediate payment / settlement of our invoice.

Wenn wir die Zahlung bis Anfang nächsten Monats nicht erhalten sind wir leider gezwungen, gerichtliche Schritte einzuleiten.	If we do not receive payment by the beginning of next month, we see no alternative but to take legal steps/action.
Wir haben die Angelegenheit unserem Rechtsanwalt übergeben.	We have placed the matter in the hands of our lawyers/solicitors.

3 Delayed payments terms

Wir hoffen auf Ihr Verständnis.	We hope you will understand our position.
Wir sind bereit, einen Zahlungsaufschub zu gewähren.	We are prepared to grant an extension.
Wir werden Ihnen eine zusätzliche Zahlungsfrist von 12 Tagen einräumen.	We shall allow you an additional period of 12 days to make payment.
Wir wären bereit, eine Teilzahlung anzunehmen.	We would be prepared to accept a part/partial payment.
Ihre Zahlungsverzögerung können wir nicht annehmen.	Your delay in payment is quite unacceptable.

4 Making and confirming payment

Die Rechnung ist verloren gegangen.	The invoice was mislaid.
Wir haben unsere Bank angewiesen, Ihnen den fälligen Betrag zu zahlen.	We have instructed our bank to pay you the outstanding amount.
Wir haben den Betrag von ... auf Ihr Konto bei der ... Bank eingezahlt/überwiesen.	We have paid/transferred/remitted the sum of ... to your account with the ... Bank.
In Begleichung / Zum Ausgleich Ihres Kontos / Ihrer Rechnung ...	In settlement of your account/invoice ...
Wir bestätigen den Eingang Ihrer Zahlung. / Wir danken Ihnen für die (schnelle) Bezahlung.	We confirm receipt of your payment. / We thank you for your (prompt) payment.
Ihre Zahlung in Höhe von ... ist bei unserer Bank eingegangen.	Your payment of ... has been received by our bank.

Dokumente gegen Akzept	documents against acceptance
per Nachnahme	C.O.D. (cash on delivery)
Zahlung im Voraus	payment in advance
Dokumentenakkreditiv (zu Ihren Gunsten)	documentary letter of credit in your favour/favor
dokumentärer Wechsel	documentary bill of exchange
unwiderruflich und bestätigt	irrevocable and confirmed
Dokumententratte	documentary draft
Zahlung bei Erhalt der Ware	payment on receipt of goods
zum gegenwärtigen Wechselkurs	at the current rate of exchange
Zahlungsempfänger	payee
zahlbar bei der ... Bank	payable at the ... bank

C Practising language

1 Fill in the missing prepositions.

> Dear Ms Foster
> Thank you ... ¹ your letter ... ² 5ᵗʰ November and your cheque ... ³ £1,000.00 ... ⁴ part settlement ... ⁵ your account. But we would like to point out that the sum still outstanding is considerable.
> As we work ... ⁶ a great extent ... ⁷ a small-profit basis, extended credit terms and the consequent loss ... ⁸ interest tends to cancel out our profit.
> ... ⁹ the circumstances you will agree that long-term credit is impracticable. We would therefore appreciate your sending us a cheque ... ¹⁰ the remaining sum ... ¹¹ £4,500.00 ... ¹² return ... ¹³ post.
> We trust you will understand our position and look forward ... ¹⁴ hearing ... ¹⁵ you soon.
> Yours sincerely

2 Complete the beginnings 1–10 with phrases a–h. Two of the items in 1–10 do not fit at all.

1. As requested we have credited your account
2. Despite our repeated requests for payment,
3. On going through our books we note
4. We are pleased to confirm
5. We request payment
6. Our invoice no. 5647G
7. Your account still shows
8. We must now insist on
9. We would like to ask you
10. If we do not receive your remittance by 16 February,

a. a debit balance of €12,375.00.
b. of the invoice total by 25 October.
c. immediate settlement of our invoice.
d. is still unpaid.
e. we have received neither your payment nor an explanation for your failure to clear your account.
f. we shall have to consider taking legal steps.
g. with the amount of $756.00.
h. that the payment of £1,275.69 clears your account.

3 Express these ideas in language that is used in business letters.

1. Sie wollen den Eingang der Rechnung CP 8796 bestätigen.
2. Sie haben Ihre Bank beauftragt, den Betrag von $1,875.00 zum Ausgleich der Rechnung zu überweisen.
3. Sie sind bereit, dem Kunden eine Verlängerung der Zahlungsfrist um 14 Tage zu gewähren.
4. Sie sagen, dass dies Ihre letzte Mahnung ist.
5. Sie sagen, dass Sie auf Ihre Bitte um Rechnungsbegleichung bisher keine Antwort erhalten haben.
6. Zur Information des Kunden legen Sie eine Rechnungskopie bei.

4 Arrange these sentences in their proper order for a reminder.

a Any further delay in payment would wipe out our small profit altogether.

b But so far we have neither received payment nor did we have a letter explaining the reasons for your delay in settling our invoice.

c Dear Mr Raumer

d We have enclosed a copy of our invoice for your information.

e Therefore, we are all the more surprised and disappointed to find that you do not seem willing to fulfil your obligations.

f Two months ago we supplied you with a variety of buttons for the tourist trade in your region.

g We wrote to you asking for payment three weeks ago.

h We look forward to hearing from you by return.

i We went out of our way to ensure that the goods reached you promptly in time for the beginning of the tourist season.

j Claire Williams

k We would like to ask you to give this matter your immediate attention and clear your account promptly.

l You will understand that the products in question are low-margin articles.

m Yours sincerely

5 Summarize the letter above.

Your boss, Herr Raumer, does not speak English very well. Summarize the main points of the letter above in German for him.

Listening Comprehension

10 6 Listen to this telephone conversation about a problem with the invoice.

Mr Loewe and Ms Matthews are discussing a problem with an invoice that has just come in. Take the part of Mr Loewe and write a note in German to the accounts department giving them the details of the telephone conversation.

GESPRÄCHSVERMERK

Für: _____   Verfasst von: _____

am: _____

Gesprächspartner: _____

Betrifft: _____

Role Play

7 Role-play the following telephone conversation with a partner.

Situation: Die Firma Textil Dorn GmbH hat Jeansstoffe an Style Four geliefert. Bei der Rechnungsstellung hat es einige Probleme gegeben.

> **Aufgabe**
> **A** ist Mitarbeiter/in von Style Four und ruft **B** von Textil Dorn an, um die Angelegenheit zu besprechen.

A	B
introduction, explains the problem, several items in recent invoice wrong	introduction, asks how he/she can help
	asks for order number and date
gives required details	
	has got the invoice on the screen, asks which items are wrong
refers to items 2, 5 and 8	
	asks for further details
item 2: invoice price seems to be higher than list price, item 5: invoiced quantity is wrong (should be 25 instead of 52); item 8 was a special offer item, invoice price is identical with list price	
	promises to settle the matter with the sales department, apologizes for the trouble
wants to know when he/she can expect a reply	
	promises to contact sales at once, thinks typing mistakes are the reason for the mistakes, hopes to phone back on the same day
asks for the matter to be put right as quickly as possible	
	apologizes once again

Payments and reminders UNIT 8

D Writing letters

1 Use the phrases below to write a reminder to a long-standing customer.
Ein langjähriger Kunde mit einer bisher ausgezeichneten Zahlungsmoral hat die Quartalsabrechnung (*quarterly statement*) von Anfang April noch nicht bezahlt. Eine erste freundliche Zahlungserinnerung von Anfang Mai ist ohne Reaktion geblieben. Jetzt, Anfang Juni, schreiben Sie erneut und bitten um Begleichung des offenen Betrags in Höhe von €25.374,75. Bieten Sie Hilfe bei der Überbrückung evtl. Schwierigkeiten an.

> **Opening**
> - We refer to our statement for the first quarter which we sent you …
> - Unfortunately, our account statement for the first quarter has not been settled yet.
> - It may be possible that our statement for the first quarter has been overlooked.
>
> **Details**
> - We sent an account statement in early April and a note asking you to settle the outstanding amount in early May.
> - So far, both our account statement from early April and our reminder of early May have gone/remained unanswered.
>
> **Action**
> - We must ask you to settle the outstanding amount without delay / by return.
> - Unless you clear your account by (date) or offer a satisfactory explanation for the delay, we will have to consider (legal) steps to recover the outstanding amount.
>
> **Close**
> - We trust that you will settle your account in the next few days.
> - If payment has already been made, please disregard this letter.

2 Write an accompanying letter for an invoice.
Teilen Sie mit, dass Sie heute eine Teillieferung (*part shipment*) aus dem Auftrag GK 2754 vom 26. Januar zum Versand bringen. Verabredungsgemäß (*as agreed*) ist eine Teilzahlung der Gesamtauftragssumme fällig. Der jetzt zu zahlende Betrag beläuft sich auf £15,000.00. Verweisen Sie auf beigefügte Rechnung. Bitten Sie um Zahlung innerhalb von 14 Tagen nach Wareneingang auf das angegebene Konto unter Angabe der Auftragsnummer. Sie gehen davon aus, dass die Ware in den nächsten Tagen wohlbehalten eintrifft.

3 Summarize the letter on the following page and write a reply.
Situation: Sie arbeiten in der Buchhaltungsabteilung der Wegener Kunststofftechnik GmbH und haben folgende Mahnung von der Beattie Engineering Ltd (24–26 Duncan Street, Sheffield SS 6 DK) erhalten.

> **Aufgabe 1**
> Machen Sie einen Vermerk über das Schreiben in Deutsch für die Abteilungsleitung.
>
> **Aufgabe 2**
> Verfassen Sie anschließend ein Antwortschreiben in Englisch unter Berücksichtigung der handschriftlichen Anmerkungen.

Wegener Kunststofftechnik GmbH
Wendenstr. 87
31226 Peine

Germany

20. September 20..

Your order no. 9630/DW for hinges

Dear Mr Stolte

We refer to am. order and our invoice no. 24680, a copy of which is enclosed for your information. Your account has been in debit for more than eight weeks now. An earlier request for the settlement of our invoice has remained unanswered and we have not received payment from you either.
You will understand that we are concerned about this situation. If you have any problems with meeting your commitments, we feel we should know about them so that we can work out a solution to your problem.
Please let us have some indication of how you are planning to proceed in this matter or, better still, transfer the full amount to clear your account.
We look forward to hearing from you in the near future.

Yours sincerely

Pamela Greer
(Accounts Dept.)

Handwritten notes:
- Bedauern für verspätete Erledigung Probleme in der Buchhaltung
- erst jetzt bekannt geworden, aber inzwischen beseitigt
- Rechnungsbetrag bereits vor Eingang des Schreiben in voller Höhe angewiesen
- Entschuldigung

4 Write a letter from notes.

Situation: Als Mitarbeiter/in der Pleiger Maschinenwerke GmbH & Co KG, Wasserbilliger Str. 34, 54294 Trier bearbeiten Sie Auslandsbestellungen. Ein neuer Kunde, Dillons Marine Engineering Ltd., 37–39 Harbour Street, Dundee DD3 8PT, dem Sie auf dessen Drängen und entgegen Ihrer Geschäftspolitik ein längeres Zahlungsziel eingeräumt hatten, hat die Rechnung über den Betrag von €15.450,68 zehn Wochen nach Rechnungsdatum noch nicht beglichen. Eine erste höfliche Zahlungserinnerung ist unbeantwortet geblieben, auch der Betrag ist nicht eingegangen.

> **Aufgabe**
> Verfassen Sie ein Mahnschreiben unter Berücksichtigung folgender Punkte:
> - Darlegung der Situation
> - Beifügung der Rechnungskopie
> - Verweis auf besonderes Entgegenkommen beim Zahlungsziel
> - Hinweis auf eigene Verpflichtungen
> - Bitte um Informationen über die Gründe des Zahlungsverzugs
> - Dringende Bitte um sofortige Überweisung des Rechnungsbetrags
> - Angemessene Schlussformel

E Unit word list

Page 82	reminder, collection letter	Zahlungserinnerung, Mahnschreiben
	invoice	Rechnung
	delayed payment terms	Zahlungsaufschub
	time allowed for payment	Zahlungsfrist
	accounting error	Fehler in der Rechnungsstellung
	discrepancy	Abweichung, Unstimmigkeit
	request for payment	Zahlungsaufforderung
	deadline for payment	Zahlungsfrist
	legal action	Klage (vor Gericht)
	to overlook	übersehen
Page 83	remittance, transfer	Überweisung
	amount due/owing, outstanding sum/amount	fälliger/offener Betrag
	to be overdue	überfällig sein
	to clear an account	Konto ausgleichen
	to transfer, to remit	überweisen
	to disregard	ignorieren
Page 84	settlement of an invoice	Rechnungsbegleichung
	delay in payment	Zahlungsverzug
	solicitor	(Rechts)Anwalt, Anwältin
Page 85	to exceed a credit period	Zahlungsfrist überschreiten / nicht beachten
	to go unnoticed	übersehen werden
	to be beyond so.'s control	etw. nicht beeinflussen können
	to meet one's (financial) obligations	seinen (Zahlungs)Verpflichtungen nachkommen
	remainder, remaining amount/sum	Restbetrag
Page 88	considerable	erheblich
	extended credit terms, long-term credit	langfristiges Zahlungsziel
	interest	Zinsen
	to cancel out	aufheben, zunichte machen
	failure	Versäumnis
Page 89	to wipe out	zunichte machen
	low-margin	mit niedriger Gewinnspanne
	to tally with	übereinstimmen mit
Page 90	typing mistake	Tippfehler
Page 91	(account) statement	Kontoaufstellung, Kontoauszug
	satisfactory	zufrieden stellend
Useful words	to adjust a mistake	einen Fehler bereinigen
	to amend an invoice	eine Rechnung berichtigen
	business dealings	Geschäftsverkehr, geschäftliche Transaktionen
	to charge	in Rechnung stellen, berechnen
	credit note	Gutschriftanzeige
	to debit	belasten

Complaints

Model letters: a complaint, reply to a complaint

Useful phrases: making a complaint (opening, saying that something has gone wrong, describing the damage, rejection of goods, solving the problem); dealing with complaints (replying to a complaint, accepting a complaint, rejecting a complaint)

Why make a complaint?

There are various reasons for making a complaint. The following are among the most frequent: delay in delivery, defective packing, wrong quality/quantity/colour/measurements, faulty goods, discrepancies between invoice and goods delivered.

Exact details about the consignment (order no., number/type of goods) should be stated. The description of the fault must also be clear, precise and comprehensive. The buyer may suggest a solution to the problem. The tone of the letter must be friendly.

Having examined the statements made by the buyer, the seller will try to put the matter right or reject the buyer's claim. The seller will always keep the business relationship with the buyer in mind. For this reason, he will often look for a compromise solution, even if he is not to blame.

How to make and reply to complaints

	Complaint	Reply to a complaint
Opening	Refer to consignment/invoice, order and goods received.	Refer to the letter of complaint and apologise.
Details	State what is wrong and give exact details.	State the results of your investigation into the problem.
Terms	Ask for replacements or reduction of invoice amount. (Ask the supplier to take back unwanted goods.)	If the problem is your fault, offer a solution (replacements, reduction of invoice amount). If not, say why not. (You may refer the buyer to the freight forwarder, insurance company etc.)
Close	(Mention the urgency of the replacement consignment.) Close with a polite ending.	(Apologise again.) Close with a polite ending.

A Model letters

1 A complaint

Fax *message*

Textil Dorn GmbH
Karlstraße 10
D-40593 Düsseldorf
Germany

62 Albert Street
London E1 5RT

Tel +44-(0)20-1724 9377
Fax +44-(0)20-1724 9388
Internet www.styfo.co.uk
Email info@styfo.co.uk

22 April 20..

Order No. 9876/P for fine corduroy material

Dear Mr Dorn

Thank you for the consignment of fine corduroy material which we received yesterday.

Unfortunately, we have reason to complain. It seems that some of the colours do not quite match the samples you sent us earlier. This is especially true of the shades of green and bordeaux red (order Nos. 4673 and 4679) which we expected to be much lighter.

While we are prepared to keep all the other items ordered, we would like to ask you to check whether we were sent the right colours for items 8 and 10 of our order. If we have been sent the wrong goods, we would appreciate receiving replacement supplies as quickly as possible.

We will hold these two items at your disposal until we hear from you and will postpone settling your invoice until the matter has been clarified.

We look forward to hearing from you by return.

Yours sincerely

Jane Adams
Buyer

Answer these questions.

1 When were the goods delivered?
2 What was wrong with the consignment?
3 Which order numbers does Ms Adams complain about?
4 What does Ms Adams ask Mr Dorn to do?
5 What is Ms Adams going to do with items 8 and 10?
6 Will the invoice be settled immediately?

2 Reply to a complaint

TextilDorn GmbH

Karlstr. 10 · D-40593 Düsseldorf

Telefon: +49-(0)211-78 34 11
Telefax: +49-(0)211-78 34 12
Email: info@textildorn.de
Internet: www.textildorn.de

FAX MESSAGE

Style Four Limited   Fax +44-(0)20-1724 9388
62 Albert Street
London E1 5RT
England

24 April 20..

Order No. 9876/P for fine corduroy material

Dear Ms Adams

Thank you for your fax message. We are sorry to read that you were not happy with the colours of the corduroy materials we sent you. We have looked into the matter very carefully and can only confirm that the colours you were sent are those that you ordered.

There may be a very simple explanation to the discrepancy in shades that you noticed. Certain colours tend to fade when exposed to strong light over a longer period. This may have occurred with the samples we sent you. We apologise for this but it certainly was not our intention to mislead you in any way.

To avoid disappointment we would, by way of exception, be willing to take back items 8 and 10. You must be aware, however, that we can not send you the lighter colouring that you prefer.
If you do not want to keep the items in question, please return them to us carriage forward. Otherwise, please settle our invoice as agreed.

We hope you can agree to this solution and look forward to hearing from you.

Yours sincerely

Jens Dorn

Find the English equivalents of these words in the fax. They are in the same order.

1 prüfen
2 bestätigen
3 Unstimmigkeit
4 Absicht
5 vermeiden
6 ausnahmsweise
7 betreffenden
8 zustimmen

B Useful phrases

1 Making a complaint

Opening

Gestern haben wir die Sendung von …, die wir am … bestellt hatten, erhalten.	We received your consignment of … yesterday which we had ordered on … / The consignment … reached us yesterday.
Gestern traf die Ware wie avisiert ein. / Ihre Sendung von … wurde gestern (an)geliefert.	Your consignment of … was delivered yesterday (as advised).
Für die Sendung von …, die gestern hier eintraf, danken wir.	(We) Thank you for your consignment of … which arrived here / which we received yesterday.

Saying that something has gone wrong

Leider hat es einen Fehler bei der Erledigung unseres Auftrags vom … gegeben.	Unfortunately, there has been an error in the handling/execution of our order No. …
Die gelieferten Artikel sind nicht die von uns bestellten / hatten wir nicht bestellt.	The goods sent/delivered are not the ones we had ordered.
Die Qualität der Waren hat unsere Erwartungen enttäuscht / nicht erfüllt.	The quality of the goods did not meet / did not come up to our expectations.

Describing the damage

Sie haben uns 500 … geschickt statt der 250, die wir bestellt hatten.	You sent us 500 … instead of the 250 which we had ordered.
Der Inhalt der Kisten stimmt nicht mit dem Packzettel / mit der Versandanzeige überein.	The contents of the crates do not agree with the packing list / delivery note.
Die Artikel sind in der falschen Farbe/Größe / sind mangelhaft.	The goods are not the colour/size we ordered / … were faulty.
In der Sendung fehlte Artikel Nr. …	Article number … was missing from the consignment.
Einige Artikel waren verkratzt / zerbrochen / (leicht) beschädigt.	Several of the items were scratched / broken / (slightly) damaged.
Die Verpackung der Ware war mangelhaft. / Die Ware war schlecht verpackt.	The goods seem to have been badly packed.

Rejection of goods

Aus diesen Gründen können wir die Waren nicht annehmen.	We cannot accept the goods for these reasons.
Wir müssen Sie bitten, uns so bald wie möglich Ersatz zu schicken.	We must ask you to send us (a) replacement(s) as soon as possible.
Wir lassen einen Teil der / die ganze Sendung an Sie zurückgehen.	We are returning part of the / the whole consignment.

Solving the problem

Wir sind bereit, die Waren (zu einem ermäßigten Preis von … das Stück) zu behalten.	We are prepared to keep the goods (at a reduced price of … per article/item).
Wir können die beschädigten Artikel nur zu einem erheblich reduzierten Preis verkaufen.	We can only sell the damaged goods at a considerably reduced price.
Wir müssen jetzt die Bestellung widerrufen.	We must now cancel our/the order.
Wir müssen um Entschädigung bitten / auf Entschädigung bestehen, um unsere Verluste zu decken.	We must ask for / insist on compensation to cover our losses.
Wir müssen Sie bitten, uns den Wert der beschädigten Waren gutzuschreiben.	We must ask you to credit us with the value of the damaged goods.
Dies hat uns erhebliche Schwierigkeiten mit einer Anzahl unserer Kunden bereitet.	This has caused us considerable difficulties/inconvenience with a number of customers.

2 Dealing with complaints

Replying to a complaint

Mit Bedauern nehmen wir Ihre Beschwerde wegen … zur Kenntnis.	We are sorry to hear that you have had reason to complain about …
Wir haben Ihre Beschwerde überprüft.	We have checked your complaint.
Da die Schäden während des Transports eingetreten sind, …	As the damage happened in transit, …

Accepting a complaint

Wir bitten vielmals um Entschuldigung für diesen Irrtum.	We offer you our sincere apologies for this error.
Wir sind bereit, die Waren gegen solche gleicher Qualität umzutauschen.	We are prepared to exchange/replace the goods for/with some of a similar quality.
Wir werden die Waren auf unsere Kosten ersetzen.	We shall replace the goods at our expense.
Wir sind bereit, Ihnen einen Nachlass von … % anzubieten.	We are prepared to offer you a reduction of …%.

Rejecting a complaint

Wir haben die Waren sehr sorgfältig überprüft und können keinen Mangel feststellen.	We have checked the goods very carefully and can find no fault with the goods.
Wir können keine Verantwortung für die Schäden übernehmen.	We cannot accept responsibility for the damage.
Wir bedauern, dass wir die Waren nicht zurücknehmen können.	We regret that we cannot take the goods back.
Wir müssen darauf hinweisen, dass die Garantiefrist abgelaufen ist.	We must point out that the period of guarantee has expired.

C Practising language

1 Use 20 of the 23 verbs from the box to fill in the missing verbs in the correct form in the sentences below.

> arrive | be | be afraid | be broken | be damaged | cause
> check | complain | ensure | find | not agree | not be packed | not match
> notice | open | order | pay | receive | return | see | send | understand

1 We ... you ... us the wrong goods.
2 The contents of case 7 ... with the packing list.
3 We ... 500 sweaters, but only ... 250.
4 When we ... the consignment, we ... that the jeans ... of the wrong sizes.
5 Unfortunately, the material ... the samples.
6 When we ... the case, we ... that item 6 from our order ... .
7 Some of the china ... because the goods ... sufficiently well.
8 We ... no alternative but to ... the goods to you.
9 Please ... that the replacement goods ... in time for the fair.
10 You ... that the delay in delivery ... us considerable inconvenience.

2 Complete the sentence beginnings 1–8 with the appropriate phrases a–j. Two of the phrases in a–j don't fit at all.

1 We accept responsibility for the damage
2 We are prepared to keep the goods
3 Your failure to supply the goods on time has caused us
4 Unfortunately, we have reason to complain
5 We have to ask for compensation
6 We offer our sincere apologies
7 In the circumstances, we are, of course, prepared to replace the goods
8 We suggest that you report the matter

a about a delay in delivery.
b at a substantially reduced price.
c at our expense.
d which must have occurred in transit.
e the consignment which arrived yesterday.
f for this error.
g to cover our losses.
h to your insurance company.
i considerable inconvenience with our customers.
j instead of 100 items.

3 The sentence parts below are in the wrong order. Rearrange them to form meaningful sentences. Add commas where necessary.

1. On examining / some of them / that / the articles / we discovered / were damp
2. After operating the machine / as expected / for a short time / we noticed / it did not perform / that
3. as proof / enclosed / For your information / of the damage / please find / some photos
4. goods / It goes / of this quality / that / to our customers / we cannot offer / without saying
5. but / have arrived / no alternative / the replacement goods / to delay payment / until / We have
6. and expense / at your risk / In the circumstances / the faulty goods / to return / we have decided
7. ask you / can be done / right / therefore / to let us know / to put the matter / We must / what
8. by at least 20 per cent / if you reduce / only be prepared / the price / to keep the goods / We will

4 Describe the charts.

As a member of a sales team, you have been involved in a survey of customer satisfaction. Your head of department is to present the two charts below at a meeting of sales directors of an international group. Describe the results of the survey as shown in the charts.

Chart 1 Complaints

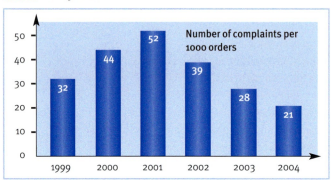

Chart 2 Customer satisfaction ratio (in percentage of respondents)

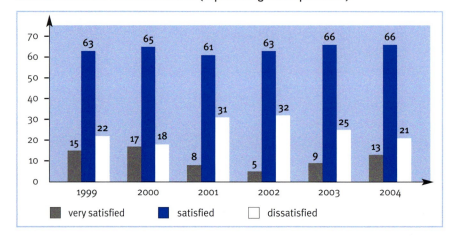

Listening Comprehension

5 **Listen to this telephone conversation about a problem with an invoice.**
Now take the part of Katja and write two separate memos in German for the accounts and dispatch departments stating what they need to do. Ask them to report back to you. Also draft an email to Helen (in English) and briefly summarize the main points of the telephone conversation.

Role Play

6 **Role-play the following conversation with a partner.**
Ihre Firma (Winter Buchvertriebsgesellschaft mbH) hat von dem irischen Lieferanten IBD (Irish Book Distributors Ltd) eine umfangreiche Sendung von Büchern für den Vertrieb in Deutschland und Österreich erhalten. Augenscheinlich ist die Sendung in mehreren Positionen unvollständig. Für Ihren Einkäufer führen Sie ein Telefonat mit dem irischen Lieferanten, um die Angelegenheit zu klären.

A	B
	Melden Sie sich mit Namen, fragen Sie, worum es geht.
Begrüßung; erklären Sie den Grund für den Anruf: Die gestern eingegangene Sendung war offenbar unvollständig.	
	Reagieren Sie erstaunt. Fragen Sie nach der Auftragsnummer auf dem Lieferschein.
Sie suchen den Lieferschein, finden ihn und lesen die Nummer vor.	
	Sie möchten den Auftrag am Bildschirm einsehen, bitten um Geduld und fragen nach den Fehlmengen.
Sie nennen Fehlmengen bei den Positionen 2 und 4, Position 12 wurde nicht geliefert.	
	Sie zeigen sich sehr erstaunt und fragen nach der Anzahl der Pakete.
Sagen Sie, dass 3 Pakete angekommen sind.	
	Erklären Sie, dass 5 Pakete vor 6 Tagen abgeschickt wurden. Schlagen Sie vor, abzuwarten, bis die restlichen Pakete eintreffen und bitten Sie dann um Rückmeldung.
Reagieren Sie überrascht. Erklären Sie sich bereit, 1–2 Tage zu warten.	
	Erwarten Sie die Rückmeldung und verabschieden Sie sich.
Verabschieden Sie sich.	

D Writing letters

1 Summarize the letter and write a complaint.

Situation: Als Assistent/in von Herrn Wolters haben Sie einem Waschmaschinen-lieferanten ein Fax wegen einer beschädigten Lieferung geschickt.

> **Aufgabe 1**
> Fassen Sie für Herrn Wolters unten stehendes Antwortschreiben von dem Lieferanten in Deutsch zusammen.
>
> **Aufgabe 2**
> Formulieren Sie die Mängelrüge, die diesem Schreiben vorausgegangen ist.

Your order for washing machines no. 1357/TS

Dear Mr Wolters

Thank you for your fax about the above-mentioned order. We were disappointed to read that some of the machines arrived scratched and that the plastic foil and cardboard covering were damaged and torn. We are now looking into the matter and have contacted our shipping company. You will understand that it will take us some time to find out how the damage could have happened. We would very much appreciate it if you could let us have a few more days to investigate the matter.

From your description of the damage and the photographs you sent us, however, it would seem that this problem may have been because of rough handling rather than poor packing. We have not had customers complain about inadequate packing before. In our opinion, such damage can only have occurred after the goods left our premises. We are now waiting for the shipping company's report and will contact you as soon as we receive it.

We are, of course, sorry that this happened at all and are confident that the matter will be settled to the satisfaction of all parties concerned.

In the meantime, we have despatched replacement machines as you need them urgently to meet your customers' orders and hope that they will arrive in good order and condition.

We will contact you again as soon as we have the shipping company's report.

Yours sincerely

Chris Bulmer
(Despatch Manager)

Complaints UNIT 9 103

2 Write a reply to this fax using the notes.

James Murray Textiles & Trading Ltd
Humberstone Business Park
18 Jameson Street
Bradford
BD6 3OP

30 June 20..

Order No. 4567/D

Dear Ms Clark

We are sorry to report that the consignment of cotton shirts despatched on 26 June (our order No. 4567/D) was delivered to us yesterday in a very unsatisfactory state. It was clear that two of the cases (Nos. 4 & 7) had been tampered with. Case No. 4 contained only 468 shirts and case No. 7 only 475 instead of the five hundred invoiced for each. Before taking the matter up with our forwarding agent, we would be grateful if you could confirm that each of these cases contained the invoiced quantity when they left your warehouse in Ashstead. At the same time, we would like you to replace the fifty-seven missing shirts with others of the same quality.

We look forward to your reply.

Yours sincerely

Anke Solms

Anke Solms
(Einkauf)

- in allen Kartons 500 Baumwollhemden jeweils nach Größen sortiert
- Kartons bei Verladung in ordentlichem Zustand
- mit bedrucktem Klebeband (tape) versiegelt (to seal)
- Spediteur hat Empfang bestätigt
- Angelegenheit wird überprüft
- Hoffnung auf baldige Klärung
- bitte kurzfristig Größen der fehlenden Hemden spezifizieren
- Nachsendung per Express möglich falls gewünscht

3 Write two emails from notes.

See the details on the following page to write two replies to this email.

```
Dear Sylvia,

We have just received and unpacked your consignment of leather
belts from our order no. 7788-DA (dated 12 January). As I couldn't
get you on the phone, I'm writing this message and hope you'll be
able to read it soon.

On checking the packing list and comparing it with our order, we
noticed that there seem to be some discrepancies in quantities
and sizes. Could I ask you to check whether there have been any
mistakes and let me know as soon as possible? We really need to
get our ranges ready and out to our customers very quickly now.

Hope to read your reply soon.

Best,

Joanne
```

Aufgabe 1
Als Sylvias Assistent/in beantworten Sie diese E-Mail. Sylvia ist auf einer dreitägigen Geschäftsreise (*on a business trip / away on business*). Prüfung soeben veranlasst; Ergebnis noch heute Vormittag erwartet; dann Rückmeldung; Bitte um Geduld; Grußformel.

Aufgabe 2
(Einige Stunden später) Bezug auf frühere E-Mail. Untersuchung zeigt Fehler beim Versand: Richtiger Packzettel wurde falscher Sendung beigelegt. Richtige Sendung bereits per Express abgeschickt, Ankunft voraussichtlich in 2 Tagen. Bitte um Rücksendung der falsch gelieferten Partie. Kosten werden selbstverständlich übernommen. Angemessene Entschuldigung.

4 Write a letter from notes.

Situation: Als Mitarbeiter/in der Einkaufsabteilung der Garten-Center Theilen GmbH, Rhedaer Str. 125, 33397 Rietberg bearbeiten Sie den Wareneingang Ausland. Ihr Unternehmen hat soeben eine umfangreiche Lieferung von elektrischen Gartengeräten der Firma Kingston Gardening Tools Ltd., 20 Hessle Street, Carlisle CA4 8GT erhalten. Der Auftrag ist insgesamt vollständig ausgeführt. Nur bei den Rasenmähern (*lawnmower*) gibt es Probleme.

Aufgabe 1
Verfassen Sie eine Mängelrüge an Kingston Gardening Tools Ltd. und berücksichtigen Sie dabei folgende Punkte:
- Auftrag Nr. 05-337/PX vom 13. des Vormonats
- Ware 10 Tage später als vereinbart eingegangen
- Erste Prüfung ergibt: Auftragsbestandteil Rasenmäher fehlerhaft: falsche Farben, Liefermenge für die verschiedenen Gerätetypen nicht gemäß Bestellung, d.h. 30 Typ HX statt 50, 40 Typ LX statt 70, aber 70 X-Plus statt 50
- Bitte um Erklärung für diese Fehllieferung und sofortige Zusendung der Fehlmengen
- Nachsendung dringend wegen bevorstehender Auslieferung an Filialen
- Wie soll mit zu viel gelieferten Geräten verfahren werden?
- Angemessener Schluss

Aufgabe 2
Als Mitarbeiter/in von Kingston Gardening Tools Ltd. bearbeiten Sie die Mängelrüge unter Berücksichtigung folgender Vorgaben:
- Bedauern wegen der aufgetretenen Probleme
- Ware pünktlich im Container abgegangen
- Nachfrage bei der Spedition (*freight forwarder*) wegen der Kürze der Zeit noch nicht beantwortet
- Diskrepanzen bei den Mengen völlig unerklärlich, möglicherweise handschriftliche Zahlen falsch gelesen
- Fehlende Mengen sind bereits versandfertig, gehen heute ab
- Spediteur hat Anweisung, zu viel gelieferte Geräte zurückzunehmen
- Entschuldigung und angemessener Schluss

E Unit word list

Page 94	complaint	Beschwerde, Mängelrüge
	to make a complaint	sich beschweren, etwas reklamieren
	to reject a complaint/claim	die Reklamation/Beschwerde zurückweisen
	delay in delivery	Lieferverzug, Verzögerung in der Auslieferung
	defective packing	schadhafte/beschädigte Verpackung
	faulty goods	fehlerhafte Waren
	to put a matter right	eine Sache berichtigen/bereinigen
	business relationship	Geschäftsbeziehung
	to be to blame	verantwortlich/schuld sein
	replacement	Ersatz(stück)
	urgency	Dringlichkeit
	replacement supply	Ersatzsendung/Ersatzlieferung
	to apologise, to offer one's apologies	sich entschuldigen
	to be s.o.'s fault	jds. Schuld sein
Page 95	corduroy	Kord(samt)
	match	übereinstimmen mit, passen zu
	to complain about	sich beschweren über
	replacement supply	Ersatzlieferung
	to hold at s.o.'s disposal	zu jds. Verfügung bereithalten
	to postpone	zurückstellen, aufschieben
Page 96	to investigate / look into a matter	Angelegenheit untersuchen
	explanation	Erklärung
	to mislead	täuschen
	disappointment	Enttäuschung
	by way of exception	ausnahmsweise
	to be aware of sth.	sich einer Sache bewusst sein
	the items in question	die betreffenden Artikel
Page 99	china	Porzellan
	to accept responsibility	die Verantwortung übernehmen
	compensation	Entschädigung
	substantially	erheblich
	to occur	geschehen
Page 100	to be disappointed (about)	enttäuscht sein (über)
	survey	Untersuchung, Überblick
Page 102	cardboard covering	Pappbedeckung
	torn	zerrissen
	rough	grob, unvorsichtig
	confident	zuversichtlich
	in good order and condition	in gutem Zustand
Page 103	to tamper with s.th.	sich an etw. zu schaffen machen
	to take a matter up with s.o.	Angelegenheit mit jdm. besprechen
Useful words	to be dissatisfied with	unzufrieden sein über
	by way of compensation (for)	als/zum Ausgleich (für)
	examination	Untersuchung, Prüfung

Applying for a job

Model letters: letter of application, CV

Useful phrases: referring to the source of information; applying for a vacancy; giving information; motivation for the new job; closing sentences

The parts of a job application

A job application is usually made up of several parts:

- the cover(ing) letter or letter of application,
- the CV (curriculum vitae) or résumé or personal data sheet (PDS) and
- certificates and testimonials (unusual in Britain or the U.S.A).

An application can be either **solicited** (the applicant replies to a job advertisement) or **unsolicited** (the applicant acts on his/her own initiative).

The cover letter and the CV are the applicant's most important selling tools. Recruiters often shortlist candidates on the basis of the information provided in these documents. Therefore they should give comprehensive information about the person, the qualifications, experience and skills of the job applicant.

How to write a letter of application
The cover letter should not be longer than about 20 lines. It has four parts:

Opening	Solicited application: refer to the job advertisement and say which job you are applying for. Unsolicited application: refer to recently obtained qualification or state reason for intended job change. Say which job you are applying for.
Qualifications and skills	State the qualifications, skills and experience that make you particularly suitable for the job.
Motivation	Write why you are applying and what you hope to achieve in the new post.
Close	State that further information can be given if necessary and when you are available for an interview. Say that you would appreciate a positive reply.

How to write a CV

The **CV** gives a full account of the candidate's education, qualifications and experience. It should be no longer than one page. **Note:** Unlike German CVs, a photo is not included in the UK or in the U.S.A. There are usually five sections in the CV:

1	Personal data	Give your address, telephone number and email address, as well as personal information: age (or date and place of birth). To prevent discrimination, there is very little personal information (i.e. regarding sex, marital status, religion) in British or American CVs.
2	Education	Give details of your school career and your college or university qualifications. State subjects and grade in final exam.
3	Job/Work experience	State where and when you trained for a job. Mention work experience including practicals or internships.
4	Skills and activities	State other qualifications and skills that may be helpful in your job (languages, IT skills, training courses relevant for the job, interests and spare time activities).
5	References	British and American CVs usually have the following sentence at the bottom of the page: "References supplied (up)on request". This is because employers do not normally write lengthy testimonials about an employee's work and abilities. Instead, they usually give a reference when asked. The applicant will give the address if necessary.

Note: CVs are not signed or dated. They often provide the information in reverse chronological order, i.e. starting with the most recent events and then going back.

Die Übersetzung kaufmännischer Berufsbezeichnungen

Es ist oft nicht einfach, eine zutreffende englische Übersetzung für kaufmännische Berufsqualifikationen zu finden. Am nächsten kommt dem Begriff „Kaufmann" bzw. „Kauffrau" die Bezeichnung „Management Assistant", die auch offiziell von den deutschen Auslandshandelskammern verwendet wird. Hier einige Beispiele:

Automobilkaufmann/-frau	Automobile Sales Management Assistant
Bankkaufmann/-frau	Bank Business Management Assistant
Bürokaufmann/-frau	Office Management Assistant
Hotelkaufmann/-frau	Management Assistant in Hotel and Hospitality
Informatikkaufmann/-frau	Management Assistant in Informatics
Industriekaufmann/-frau	Industrial Business Management Assistant
IT-System-Kaufmann/-frau	Management Assistant in IT systems
Kaufmann/-frau im Einzelhandel	Management Assistant in Retail Business
Kaufmann/-frau im Groß- und Außenhandel	Management Assistant in Wholesale and Foreign Trade
Reiseverkehrskaufmann/-frau	Travel Management Assistant
Veranstaltungskaufmann/-frau	Management Assistant in Event Organisation
Versicherungskaufmann/-frau	Insurance Business Management Assistant
Werbekaufmann/-frau	Management Assistant in Advertising

Model letters and CVs

1 Letter of application

Timo Sanders writes a cover letter for his application for a work placement.

Timo Sanders

Alte Landstr. 17
45875 Gelsenkirchen
Tel. 02 09/48 62 48
mobile: 0160/27 34 987
email: timosanders1@gmx.de

Northumberland Farm Supplies Ltd
Morpeth Branch
17 North Morpeth Business Park
Morpeth
Northumberland
NE62 4RD
England

12 January 20..

Application for a work placement

Dear Sir or Madam

A work placement abroad is strongly recommended for students of business administration at the Gelsenkirchen Polytechnic. Therefore, I am planning to do such a placement during the summer break this year and would like to ask you to consider my application for a three-month placement in your company.

I obtained your address from the WCG (a farm supplies distributor) here in Münster where I completed a vocational training of two and a half years before taking up business administration at Gelsenkirchen Polytechnic. As I am familiar with the trade of products for the farming community here in Germany, I would like to gain experience in a similar field in Britain.

As you will see from the enclosed CV, I am a fully qualified Management Assistant in Wholesale and Foreign Trade. I am able to familiarise myself with computer applications very quickly and have a good command of English. Business English is an integral component of our degree course.

If possible, I would like to join your firm for the summer months, ideally for the period from 1 July to 30 September, but other periods would also be possible. Should you have any further queries, please do not hesitate to contact me by phone or mail.

I would be pleased to be able to work in Morpeth and look forward to your reply.

Yours faithfully

Timo Sanders

Enclosures

Answer these questions.

1 What are students of business administration expected to do?
2 For how long does Timo plan to go to Britain?
3 What did Timo do at the WCG for two and a half years?
4 What qualification did Timo get at the end of his training?
5 How good is Timo's English?
6 When is Timo planning to come to Britain?

2 CV

Here is the CV that Timo sends together with the cover letter.

Timo Sanders

Alte Landstr. 17
45875 Gelsenkirchen
Tel. 02 09/48 62 48
mobile: 0160/27 34 987
email: timosanders1@gmx.de

Curriculum vitae

PERSONAL DATA
Born: 31 October 1981 in Bremen
Nationality: German
Marital status: Single

EDUCATION
1987–1991   Primary school in Bremen
1991–1997   Comprehensive school in Bremen
                   School-leaving certificate (corresponds to GCSE)
1997–1999   College of Commerce in Münster
                   Fachabitur (corresponds to A-levels)
                   Average grade: 2.3
Since 2001   Gelsenkirchen Polytechnic
                   4-year course in Business Management

WORK EXPERIENCE
1998–1999   WCG Münster – part-time work (assisting in the warehouse)
1999–2001   WCG Münster – vocational training as Management
                   Assistant in Wholesale and Foreign Trade
Spring 2001   Qualifying examination for Management Assistant in
                   Wholesale and Foreign Trade at the
                   Münster Chamber of Commerce and Industry (IHK)
                   Final grade: 1.7 (89%)

ACTIVITIES AND QUALIFICATIONS
2001–2002   Community service (meals-on-wheels unit of the local Red
                   Cross branch)
Languages   English – good (some knowledge of business English)
                   French – fair
                   Spanish – beginner

Computer literacy Familiar with standard software programs
                   (MS Office, Lotus, Linux)

Activities   Handball, also coaching a boys' team at C-level
                   Member of the Gelsenkirchen Polytechnic student
                   representative council

References can be supplied upon request.

**Find the English equivalents of the following in the CV.
They are not necessarily in the same order.**

a Durchschnittsnote
b Gesamtschule
c Lager
d Abschlusszeugnis
e Groß- und Außenhandelskaufmann
f Teilzeit

B Useful phrases

1 Referring to the source of information

Vom Arbeitsamt / Von der Berufsberatung habe ich erfahren, dass Sie … einstellen / eine Stelle als … zu besetzen haben.	I have learned from the job centre / careers office that you are recruiting … / have a vacancy for …
In der gestrigen/heutigen Ausgabe / In der Ausgabe vom … der/des … (Titel der Zeitung/ Zeitschrift) haben Sie die Stelle einer/eines … ausgeschrieben.	You advertised the post/position of … in yesterday's/today's issue / in the issue of … of …
Ihre Anzeige letzte Woche im / in der … habe ich mit Interesse gelesen, …	I was interested to read your advertisement in last week's edition of the …

2 Applying for a vacancy

Ich möchte mich um die ausgeschriebene Stelle bewerben.	I wish to apply / I would like you to consider my application for the advertised post.
Wie in unserem heutigen Telefonat verabredet/ besprochen übersende ich Ihnen hiermit meine Bewerbungsunterlagen.	Following our telephone conversation / As discussed on the phone today, I am sending you my application.
Nach Abschluss meiner Ausbildung als … / meines Studiums in … suche ich nach einer Beschäftigung in …	Having completed my training / university course in … , I am now looking for a post in …

3 Giving information

Wie Sie aus dem beiliegenden Lebenslauf ersehen, …	As you will see from the enclosed curriculum vitae / resume / profile, …
Gegenwärtig/Zurzeit bin ich bei einer Import- firma / als Fremdsprachenkorrespondentin in einer Großhandelsfirma beschäftigt.	I am currently working for an import firm / as a foreign language correspondent in a wholesaling company.
Ich habe / verfüge über umfassende Computer- kenntnisse / Erfahrung im Kundendienst.	I am computer-literate. / I have a lot of experience in customer services.
Ich spreche fließend Englisch und Spanisch und habe Grundkenntnisse in Französisch.	I speak fluent English and Spanish / English and Spanish fluently and have a basic knowledge of French.
Ich bin in … qualifiziert / habe ein Diplom / einen akademischen Grad in …	I have qualifications / a diploma / a degree in …
… wo ich … als Hauptfach (mit… als Nebenfach) studierte.	… where I studied … as my main subject [US: my major] (and … as my subsidiary subject [US: my minor]).

... habe ich das Examen in den folgenden Fächern bestanden: ...	... I graduated in the following subjects: ...
Nach der Berufsausbildung war ich vier Jahre bei einer ortsansässigen Exportfirma tätig.	After my (vocational) training, I worked for a local export firm for four years.
Während des Studiums habe ich zwei Praktika im Ausland absolviert / gemacht.	During my studies, I did two work placements / practicals abroad.
Ich habe eine Ausbildung als ... / Ich wurde als zweisprachige Sekretärin / Fremdsprachenkorrespondentin ausgebildet.	I was trained as a bilingual / foreign-language secretary.

4 Motivation for the new job

Ich suche eine ähnliche Stelle mit mehr Verantwortung / mit Aufstiegsmöglichkeiten.	I am looking for a similar post with more responsibility / promotion prospects.
In der ausgeschriebenen Position hoffe ich, meine Kompetenzen / Erfahrung in ... anwenden / einsetzen / einbringen zu können.	I hope to / I am confident that I will be able to use / apply my skills / experience in ... in the advertised post.
Die Arbeit mit ... hat mich schon während meiner Ausbildung interessiert.	I have taken a great interest in working (together) with ... during my training.
Jetzt möchte ich meine Stelle wechseln / für ein größeres Unternehmen arbeiten.	I now wish to change my job / to work for a larger organisation.
Ich möchte im Ausland arbeiten und meine Fremdsprachenkenntnisse anwenden.	I wish to work abroad and to make use of my knowledge of languages.

5 Closing sentences

Meinen Lebenslauf und Kopien meiner Zeugnisse finden Sie in der beigefügten Mappe. / Beigefügt finden Sie ...	You will find my CV and copies of my diplomas / certificates enclosed.
Sollten Sie weitere Informationen über meine Person und meine Qualifikationen benötigen, bin ich gern bereit Referenzen anzugeben.	Should you require further information about my person or my qualifications, I would be pleased to quote references.
In der Anlage finden Sie die Namen von zwei Personen, die bereit sind, jede gewünschte Auskunft über mich zu geben.	The names of two referees [US: references] are given below.
Für ein Vorstellungsgespräch stehe ich jederzeit gern zur Verfügung.	I am available for an interview at any time.
Über die Einladung zu einem persönlichen Gespräch würde ich mich sehr freuen.	I would be grateful for / appreciate the opportunity to present myself in an interview.

C Practising language

1 Decide which does not fit into the group.

1	a receptionist	b telephonist	c stockist	d typist
2	a accounts manager	b human resources manager	c personnel officer	d recruiter
3	a buying clerk	b chief buyer	c purchasing manager	d warehouse manager
4	a advertising agent	b product manager	c sales assistant	d sales representative
5	a deputy manager	b office clerk	c personal assistant	d secretary
6	a builder	b fitter	c maintenance engineer	d technician

2 Replace the terms in *italics* by suitable ones from the box below. There are more terms than you need.

> a candidate | activities | advertisement | available | believe | challenging
> completing | continued | customers | department | experience | helpful
> interest | interview | issue | references | standard | testimonials | training

I was interested to see your *announcement*¹ for the post of a junior export sales officer in the June *copy*² of "Trade International" and I would like to be considered as *an applicant*³ for that vacancy.

I *feel*⁴ I am fully qualified for the post as after *ending*⁵ my course in business studies at Kingston College of Further Education, I worked in the sales *section*⁶ of a small local wholesale business. My *tasks*⁷ there involved dealing with *business contacts*⁸ at home and abroad. I am familiar with the *traditional*⁹ office communication facilities. At college, I *carried on* with¹⁰ French and also learnt some Spanish.

I am keen to do some more *demanding*¹¹ work and feel that the experience gained in my present job will be *useful*¹² in your company.

My CV and the usual *certificates*¹³ are enclosed.

I am *ready*¹⁴ for a personal *discussion*¹⁵ at your convenience and look forward to hearing from you.

3 Reorganise the parts in the proper order to form full sentences. Choose the correct forms of the verbs.

1 as a management assistant / I / in human resources / train with / Wolters Maschinenbau GmbH
2 as an assistant to the area sales manager / for two years / I / in Swansea / work
3 additional courses / as a management assistant in insurance / attend / during my training / I / to improve my computing skills
4 as a management assistant / complete / in property management / in two months' time / I / my training
5 as a temp / I / in the logistics department / of IPEX Mediatechnik GmbH / since leaving school / work
6 as a management assistant / in wholesaling and retailing / last / my training / three years
7 for an opening in an engineering company / having completed / I / in office communication / look / my training
8 after my traineeship / continue / I / in the capacity of field representative / to work / with Steinmeyer & Partners / with this company

4 Use the ideas in brackets to complete these sentences.

1 The advertisement on your website for the post of bilingual sales manager … (*interest me*)
2 I am interested in applying for the advertised vacancy and … (*enclose personal profile*)
3 As an experienced administrative assistant, … (*meet requirements*)
4 I believe that I have the necessary drive and team spirit … (*contribute to business success*)
5 My present job involves a lot of keyboarding activities. Therefore, … (*familiarity with word processing software*)
6 Having gained experience in a small but busy office, … (*seek new challenge*)
7 I feel that, with my foreign language skills, … (*contribute to international sales efforts*)
8 I would welcome the opportunity … (*come for an interview*)
9 Should you require any further information, … (*phone or mail*)
10 If necessary … (*supply references*)

5 Rewrite the cover letter on the following page to avoid the repetition of *I*-structures. Go back to the Useful phrases section (Part B of this Unit) and read the suggestions in the box below for ideas.

- Having graduated …
- Having seen …
- In the position of …, I …
- In your advertisement …
- That is why / Therefore I …
- You can reach me…
- You can see …

> ### Application for post of PA
>
> I saw your advertisement for the post of PA in yesterday's issue of the New York Times. I would like to apply for this post and am sending you my CV as an enclosure.
>
> I am confident that I meet your requirements as I have recently graduated from Albany Secretarial College. I have good keyboarding skills (50 wpm) and shorthand skills (40 wpm). I gained some experience as a secretary at Ogilvy & Partners (a law firm) where I did a lot of copy-typing.
>
> I am now seeking a new challenge in an office with more direct client contact and more responsible work. I would like to make better use of the foreign language skills I acquired at school and in evening classes. I am also familiar with the standard software programs. I would very much enjoy becoming part of an active team-oriented environment.
>
> I will be happy to supply any supplementary information you require and am available for an interview at any time.
>
> I can be contacted by phone or email and I look forward to your reply.

Role Play

6 Interview your partner.

In a job interview, the interviewee is usually asked about points like career at school/university, job training, work experience, special skills and previous employers.

a Think of questions the interviewer might ask. Consider some of the following points:
- school qualifications
- stays abroad (where, for how long)
- skills other than those acquired at school, e.g. language or IT
- job training (special area, where, how long, which company department, job content)
- company profile (type of company, size, product range, markets)

b With a partner, role-play an interview for a job.

Interviewer: Use some of the points raised in **a** above to find out as much about your partner as you can. Try to follow a logical sequence but also take up points made by the interviewee.

Interviewee: Use your own personal profile to answer the interviewer's questions. Give more detailed information whenever suitable.

Listening Comprehension

 7 Listen to the telephone message and take notes. Pass the information on to your neighbour.

Sheila takes a telephone message for her brother Roger and tells him about an appointment for an interview when he comes home later in the evening. Write a note to Roger including the following details:
- who called and why
- contact details
- information about the appointment and where to go

Writing letters and CVs

1 Decide which of the terms and expressions in *italics* are suitable for a cover letter. Work in groups.

1 I was interested to see your *advertisement / announcement / commercial / information* [a] for the *job / place / post / position* [b] of an event manager and I *plan / want / wish / would like* [c] to *apply / be considered / be chosen / stand* as a candidate [d].
2 As you will *see / note / notice / remark* [a] from my *CV / factsheet / profile / resume* [b], I have the *asked for / demanded / necessary / required* [d] *certificates / exams / qualifications / tests* [c] to meet your *claims / demands / requests / requirements* [e].
3 After *attending / going to / leaving / visiting* [a] *driving school / college / university / the polytechnic* [b] I *learnt the job of / studied the work of / trained as / was educated as* [c] a singer.
4 I *gained / had / made / obtained* [a] some *experience / information / knowledge / skills* [b] in an advertising *agency / company / bureau / office* [c] and I would now like *to get to know / to know / to learn about / to see* [d] the *function / job / task / work* [e] of a public relations *branch / department / office / section* [f].
5 *If / Should / When / Whenever* [a] you require *additional / better / further / more* [b] information, please do not hesitate to *call / contact / inform / tell* [c] me.

2 Put these sentences in the proper order for a cover letter.

Dear Mr. Henderson:

a An interview can be arranged at any time.
b I will have completed my two-year training as an office assistant with Hunters Corp here in Portland by the end of June.
c But as my company has no opening for me, I am now looking for opportunities to use my skills elsewhere.
d During my traineeship, I also attended evening classes in office management, computing and general secretarial duties.
e You will see from my resume and certificates that I have already gained some work experience in the sector in which you operate.
f I am confident that my training and the skills I acquired at college make me suitable for such a position.
g I found your address in the career centre's job file and wish to apply for the advertised post of junior office assistant.
h I look forward to hearing from you.
i If you require any additional information, please do not hesitate to contact me by phone or mail.
j I hope to gain further experience and to make a positive contribution to the success of your business.

Yours truly,

3 Reassemble the information below for a CV.

Use the following headings:
Personal data; Education; Work experience; Activities and interests.

1990–1993	Primary school in Munich
1993–2002	Grammar school in Munich, Abitur (average grade 2.3)
1999–2000	6 months exchange visit to Seaford sixth form college
2002-present	Traineeship at Hypo- und Vereinsbank (HVB) in Munich

80021 Munich
Born on 21 November 1984 in Kempten
Christina Voigt
Computer literacy
Curriculum vitae
E-Mail tinavoigt@t-online.de
English – fluent

July 2001	1 month's work experience at Barclay's Bank London – customer services department

Familiar with standard software programs
Female
French – fairly fluent
Interests
Languages
Reading, riding, travelling, meeting people
References supplied upon request
Robert-Koch-Str. 15
Single
Tel. 089/49 50 819

4 Applying for a job in a temping agency.

Refer to your telephone conversation with someone from a temping agency and write a cover letter for your application for one of these office jobs.

Positions	Requirements
Executive assistant	1 year office experience
Legal assistant	MS Office skills
Bilingual secretary	foreign languages
Receptionist	friendly personality
	good communicative skills
	able to work under pressure

5 Write a cover letter and a CV.

Write a cover letter and CV based on your own personal profile (school career, work experience, activities, skills, interests) to apply for a 3-month work placement in a field of your choice.

E Unit word list

Page 106	to apply for a job/vacancy/post	*sich um eine (freie) Stelle bewerben*
	job application	*Stellenbewerbung*
	cover(ing) letter	*Bewerbungsschreiben*
	CV (curriculum vitae), résumé, personal data sheet (PDS)	*Lebenslauf*
	certificate	*Bescheinigung; hier: Zeugnis*
	testimonial, reference	*Referenz, Empfehlungsschreiben*
	advertisement	*Anzeige*
	unsolicited application	*Initiativ-, Blindbewerbung*
	(vocational) qualification	*(Berufs)Bildungsabschluss*
	skills	*Fertigkeiten, Kompetenz*
Page 107	(work) experience	*(Berufs)Erfahrung, (praktische) Erfahrung*
	(job) interview	*Vorstellungsgespräch*
	(to do) an internship, a work placement	*ein Praktikum (machen)*
	IT (information technology) skills, computer literacy	*EDV-Kenntnisse*
	to supply an address / information / a reference	*eine Anschrift / eine Referenz angeben/ mitteilen, Informationen liefern*
Page 108	polytechnic	*Fachhochschule*
	vocational training	*(Berufs)Ausbildung*
	to gain experience	*Erfahrungen machen/sammeln*
	good command of a language	*gute Sprachkenntnisse*
	degree course	*Studiengang*
Page 109	school-leaving certificate	*Abschlusszeugnis*
	GCSE	*(entspricht) Mittlere Reife*
	A-levels *[GB]*	*(entspricht) Abitur*
	part-time work	*Teilzeitarbeit*
	qualifying examination	*Ausbildungsabschlussprüfung*
	community service	*Zivildienst*
Page 112	stockist	*Fachhändler, Fachgeschäft*
	accounts	*Buchhaltung(sabteilung)*
	human resources	*Personal(abteilung)*
	purchasing	*Einkauf(sabteilung)*
	deputy	*Vertretungs-*
	fitter	*Monteur*
	maintenance	*Wartung*
Page 113	in the capacity of a(n)	*in der Eigenschaft einer/s*
	field representative	*Außenvertreter/in*
	traineeship	*(kaufmännische) Ausbildung*
Page 114	job training	*Ausbildung*
Page 115	to attend a course	*einen Kurs besuchen*
	branch	*Filiale, Zweigstelle*
Useful words	apprentice(ship)	*Lehrling (Lehre) in einem gewerblichen Beruf*
	temp; temping	*Zeitarbeiter/in; Zeitarbeit, Leiharbeit*
	trainee	*Auszubildende/r in einem kaufmännischen Beruf*

Musterprüfungen

Allgemeines zu den Prüfungen

Während die Prüfung *Fremdsprache im Beruf (FIB) I* eher für Berufspraktiker gedacht ist, dürfen an der *Zusatzqualifikation Fremdsprache für kaufmännische Auszubildende* nur Auszubildende teilnehmen.

Die folgenden Prüfungssätze decken nur den schriftlichen Teil der beiden Prüfungen ab. Neben den fünf schriftlichen gibt es noch zwei mündliche Aufgaben, die unten näher beschrieben werden.

Schriftlicher Teil

Aufgaben 1–3

Die schriftlichen Aufgaben sind in beiden Prüfungen in Bezug auf Form, Inhalt und Anforderungsprofil teilweise identisch.
So muss in beiden zuerst ein Geschäftsbrief und dann eine E-Mail verfasst werden, und zwar jeweils auf Englisch nach Angaben in Deutsch. Anschließend soll ein Telefongespräch auf Deutsch zusammengefasst werden, bei dem den Kandidaten die Äußerungen eines der beiden Gesprächspartner, aus dessen Sicht sie dann das Gespräch wiedergeben müssen, vorliegt. Hierbei handelt es sich um einen Vermerk, etwa in Form eines Memos, bei dem allerdings ganze Sätze verwendet werden sollen.

Aufgabe 4

Hier geht es wieder um eine Zusammenfassung. Grundlage dazu bildet in der *FIB I*-Prüfung ein branchenspezifischer Sachtext, der unter Beachtung der Leitfragen in der Aufgabenstellung auf ca. 1/3 der Länge gekürzt werden muss. Wichtig ist hierbei die Reduzierung auf relevante Informationen. Für die Zusammenfassung von Sachtexten gibt es in diesem Buch kein vorbereitendes Material, da dazu jeder in Thema, Umfang und Niveau geeignete Artikel aus dem Wirtschaftsteil einer englischsprachigen Zeitung oder andere branchenspezifische Sachtexte verwendet werden können.

In der Prüfung *Zusatzqualifikation* geht es in dieser Aufgabe darum, einen Vermerk über einen Geschäftsbrief für einen Dritten abzufassen, bei dem die wesentlichen Informationen verständlich und prägnant herausgefiltert werden müssen.

Aufgabe 5

Während der schriftliche Teil in der *FIB I*-Prüfung mit einer Beschreibung bzw. Auswertung eines Diagramms, einer Grafik o.Ä. abschließt, müssen die Kandidaten für die *Zusatzqualifikation* einen Sprachergänzungstext absolvieren. Dieser besteht aus zwei Teilen, einem Lückentext mit (überzähligen) Vorgaben zum Einsetzen und einer Multiple-Choice-Aufgabe.

Mündlicher Teil

Der mündliche Teil gliedert sich in zwei Abschnitte, die zusammen 30 Minuten in Anspruch nehmen. Zunächst wird ein Gespräch in der Fremdsprache geführt, bei dem es um allgemeine Dinge und geschäftlichen Smalltalk geht. Typische Fragen wären etwa:

- *Can you tell us something about yourself and your personal interests? (Age, where you are from, where you live, hobbies)*
- *Now can you please tell us about the company you work for and what you do there?*
  (The answer should include information on:
  – the company size, products, customers and if possible competitors
  – the name of the apprenticeship / trainee scheme.)
- *Please tell us something about your apprenticeship.*
  (The answer should include names of different departments, when the apprenticeship began, when it will finish.)
- *Which department did you like best and why?*
- *What are your plans for the future, for when you finish your apprenticeship?*
- *What are some of the things you had to do in the different departments?*
  (Information on typical order processing and other commercial activities)

Der zweite Teil besteht aus einem Telefongespräch, das der Kandidat mit einem Prüfer durchführt. Anhand von schriftlichen Vorgaben geht es um Themen aus dem beruflichen Alltag, etwa Terminabsprachen, Wegbeschreibungen, das Organisieren einer Konferenz, Anfragen, Bestellungen, Lieferungen oder Nachfragen zu Sachverhalten (z. B. Rechnungen, Lieferungen, Bestellungen, technische Daten oder Termine).

Fremdsprache im Beruf (FIB) I

1
Geschäftsbrief in der Fremdsprache nach Angaben in Deutsch (Bearbeitungszeit 45 Minuten)

Situation: Als Mitarbeiter/in der Feldhaus Metall GmbH, Bergmannstr. 69, 09131 Chemnitz ist es Ihre Aufgabe, den Zahlungseingang zu überwachen. Der amerikanische Kunde Williams & Cross Telekom Inc., 123 Light Street, Freemont, MI 44403 hat trotz zweimaliger Zahlungsaufforderung seine Rechnung in Höhe von € 20.485,64 noch nicht beglichen. Ihre Firma war dem Kunden in Bezug auf Konditionen und Lieferzeiten über das übliche Maß hinaus entgegengekommen.

Aufgabe: Schreiben Sie eine dritte und letzte Zahlungserinnerung und berücksichtigen Sie dabei folgende Punkte:
- Verweis auf Auftragsnummer und Rechnungsnummer sowie zwei bisher erfolglose Zahlungserinnerungen
- Hinweis auf ausnahmsweise gewährte günstige Preise und Rabatte für diesen Auftrag
- Hinweis auf besonders schnelle Erledigung
- Bei Zahlungsschwierigkeiten bitte um Mitteilung, dann Versuch einer Lösung
- Bitte um sofortige Begleichung (Frist: 14 Tage nach Briefeingang) – Rechnungskopie beiliegend
- Nach Fristablauf Einschaltung des Rechtsanwalts

2
Informelle schriftliche Mitteilung in der Fremdsprache als Reaktion auf eine fremdsprachige Vorlage (Bearbeitungszeit 30 Minuten)

Situation: Als Mitarbeiter/in in der Abteilung Marktanalyse der Heinemann Consulting GmbH & Co KG, Kölner Str. 28, 51429 Bergisch Gladbach (hartmut.meister@heinemannconsult.de) hatten Sie einen Besuchstermin bei dem amerikanischen Kunden Waters Financial Services Inc., 45 West Main Street, Nashville, TN 37211 (dennis.alsan@watersfinance.com.us) vereinbart, um die Ergebnisse Ihrer Marktanalyse vorzustellen. Dieser Termin sollte in 14 Tagen stattfinden. Die beiliegende E-Mail erfordert eine Terminänderung.

Aufgabe: Beantworten Sie diese E-Mail und berücksichtigen Sie dabei folgende Punkte:
- nicht erfreut über die Verlegung, Zeit für die Vorbereitung des Berichts und der Präsentation nun sehr kurz
- Versuch, das durch Überstunden auszugleichen
- Erfolg beim Umbuchen des Flugs (Ankunft in Chicago ca. 15.00 Uhr Ortszeit)
- Dank für Hilfe bei Hotelbuchung (3 Einzelzimmer erforderlich)
- Bitte um Mitteilung, wann Präsentation beginnen soll
- Möglichkeit, Bericht evtl. noch vor der Präsentation zu kopieren?

Heinemann Marketing Dept.

Change of schedule

Dear Hartmut

I'm writing to inform you that, unfortunately, we need to reschedule our meeting that we had planned to take place in two weeks' time. Our vice-president from head office in Cincinnati has indicated a keen interest in your presentation and asked me to try and get the date for the meeting changed, i.e. put forward by 4 days. The only day he has available is Thursday, March 2nd. I know this may be very awkward for you as you will be wanting to put the finishing touches on your report and the presentation. On the other hand, you will only lose two working days. I reckon reorganising travel might be the biggest problem. Let us know as quickly as possible whether you can make it. It is very important for us, and perhaps for you too, that head office is showing an interest.

I hope you can change your travel booking. As soon as we know your answer, we will make the necessary arrangements here at this end (hotel etc.). So you needn't worry on that count.

Best wishes

Dennis

3

Vermerk in Deutsch über ein in der Fremdsprache dargebotenes Gespräch / eine in der Fremdsprache dargebotene mündliche Mitteilung
(Bearbeitungszeit 30 Minuten)

Situation: Sie sind Frau Berger und führen ein Telefonat mit einem irischen Lieferanten. In der letzten Rechnung gibt es ein paar Unstimmigkeiten zu klären.

Aufgabe: Sie hören das Gespräch zweimal. Fertigen Sie anschließend eine Zusammenfassung für Ihre Abteilungsleitung an.

...

Berger: Good morning. This is Tanja Berger from Maurer Systeme KG in Karlsruhe in Germany.

...

Berger: Well, I'm phoning about your invoice AM 2602 which we received a couple of days ago.

...

Berger: Well, you see, there seem to be one or two problems.

...

Berger: Yes, certainly. Well, it's AM 2602.

...

Berger: Just a second. – Oh, here it is. It's G for Golf, and then the number is 11 08 99.

...

Berger: That's right. Well, you see ...

...

Berger: Fine. Well, as I said the problem is that in one or two cases, the prices in your invoice are not those in your catalogue on the basis of which we ordered.

...

Berger: Yeah, sure. Well, item 3 for example. Your price is €15.54 per unit whereas the catalogue says €15.45. And then there is item 7. Here, your price per unit is €21.87 and the catalogue price is €21.78.

...

Berger: Your latest spring catalogue, of course.

...

Berger: Sorry, but I've got a couple more points. For item 13 the invoice states 500 pieces, but we only received 300 which is also the number we ordered.

...

Berger: And then we had a credit note for €233.75 from you three weeks ago. But I can't see that the amount has been deducted from the invoice total.

...

Berger: Yeah, here we are. So the number is 200334–K, and the date is 10 June.

...

Berger: No, no. The number is 200334–K

...

Berger: The date was 10 June.

...

Berger: Looks like it, doesn't it?

...

Berger: That's it, exactly.

...

Berger: OK. That sounds like a good solution. Thanks for your help.

...

Berger: Bye.

4

Gelenkte Zusammenfassung in Deutsch eines fremdsprachigen Texts von 200 bis 250 Wörtern
(Bearbeitungszeit 45 Minuten)

Aufgabe: Fassen Sie diesen Text zusammen und berücksichtigen Sie dabei die folgenden Punkte:
- Gegenwärtige Situation in Großbritannien
- Zukunft der „pubs"
- Situation in anderen Märkten

Across Europe, people are drinking more alcohol at home and less in bars and pubs – a quiet shift in behaviour that presents a big challenge to brewers and other drinks multinationals. The trend is particularly marked among the British, a nationality previously noted for herd-drinking at public watering holes. The country's 60,000 pubs still form the heart of many villages and suburbs, but their role is changing as more people drink beer from cans in their living rooms.

It is thought that, by 2007 or 2008, the UK will be buying most of its beer from supermarkets and other stores instead. Most of it will be drunk at home. Many pubs have insured themselves against this trend by selling more food. One important factor in the growth in home drinking has been the near-disappearance of miners, steelworkers and other blue-collar employees who were the most regular and heavy bar users in the past.

In Ireland, the on-trade market, which consists of all alcoholic drinks sold through pubs, bars and restaurants, declined by 8 per cent in the second half of 2003, while off-trade sales through shops and supermarkets rose by 3 per cent.

In France, too, the on-trade is down dramatically. The decline follows a long police campaign aimed at reducing drink-driving. Yet there are also signs of a shift in French consumer preferences when it comes to drinking venues. The proportion of beer sold through shops in France, Germany and Spain has grown steadily at the expense of bars.

(250 words)

5

Gelenkte fremdsprachige schriftliche Beschreibung visuellen Materials (z.B. Grafiken, Organigramme, Tabellen, Flussdiagramme, Pläne)
(Bearbeitungszeit 30 Minuten)

Aufgabe: Beschreiben Sie dieses Diagramm in Englisch und stellen Sie die Veränderung im Bierkonsum zu Hause dar.

Europe gains a taste for drinking beer at home
% bought in shops and supermarkets

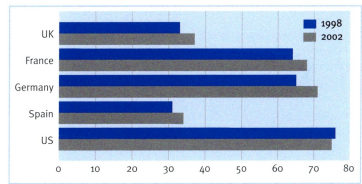

Zusatzqualifikation Fremdsprache für kaufmännische Auszubildende

1
Geschäftsbrief in der Fremdsprache nach Stichwortangaben in Deutsch (Bearbeitungszeit 45 Minuten)

Situation: Als Mitarbeiter/in der Firma Maschinenbau Zilinski GmbH, Leschwitzer Str. 47, 02827 Görlitz, bearbeiten Sie den Auftrag der Johnstone Engineering Inc., 7535 Paterson Drive, Baltimore, Maryland, MD 21354, U.S.A.

Aufgabe: Bestätigen Sie sich den Auftrag auf die Lieferung von Hebewerkzeugen (*lifting gear*) für Warenlager (*warehouse*) und gehen Sie dabei auf folgende Punkte ein:

- Dank für den umfangreichen Auftrag
- Umgehende Bearbeitung
- Wegen des Umfangs Anlieferung zum gewünschten Termin problematisch
- Vorschlag: Lieferung in 2 Partien (*lot*) ohne zusätzliche Kosten für den Kunden, erste Partie wie vereinbart 3 Wochen nach Auftragserteilung, zweite Partie 14 Tage später
- Sonstige Konditionen unverändert, d.h. Zahlung in 2 gleichen Raten (*instalment*) bei Auftragserteilung und 14 Tage nach Lieferung
- Bitte um Verständnis und Zustimmung zu diesem Vorschlag

2

Kurz gefasste schriftliche Mitteilung per moderner Telekommunikation zu einem in der Fremdsprache vorgegebenen Geschäftsfall (Bearbeitungszeit 30 Minuten)

Situation: Als Mitarbeiter/in der Geschäftsleitung der Beinheim Maschinenbau GmbH, Düsseldorfer Str. 76, 40764 Langenfeld, koordinieren Sie die Besuchstermine. Für den Anfang der Woche war ein umfangreiches Besuchsprogramm für eine Delegation der Technomot Clairet S.A.R.L., Dünkirchen vorgesehen. Auf der E-Mail von Technomot Clairet hat die Geschäftsleitung Anweisungen notiert.

Aufgabe: Beantworten Sie die E-Mail unter Berücksichtigung der Vorgaben der Geschäftsleitung.

Jennings@Beinheim-maschinen.de

Visit of project team

Dear Mr. Jennings

Thank you very much for sending us the schedule for our project team's visit so early. Our chief engineer, M. François Legrand, and our marketing manager, M. Etienne Miraud, will also be part of the team to discuss details regarding the production and distribution of the new gearboxes (*Kupplungsgehäuse*). Both these gentlemen, however, will only be able to join our team in the second half of the week, i.e. on Thursday, 24 June.
Therefore, we would appreciate it if you could reschedule the meetings with your management so that top-level negotiations can be started on that day.
We have attached a first draft for the production schedule for our works here in Dunkirk for your information along with an assessment of the current market situation here in France. This could provide a basis for our discussions.
We hope that the change of arrangements will meet with your approval and would like to ask you to make the necessary hotel bookings. Thank you in advance for your understanding and we are looking forward to hearing from you by return.

Best wishes

Denise Guillot

Handschriftliche Notizen:
- erfreut über Beteiligung beider Herren
- Dank für Vorlagen, sehr nützlich
- Termine bestätigen
- Arbeitsplan entsprechend ändern
- Hotelbuchung vornehmen und bestätigen
- Gespräche mit Geschäftsführung am 24.6. (nachmittags)
- Besuchsprogramm für das Wochenende ankündigen

3

Vermerk in Deutsch über ein in der Fremdsprache dargebotenes Gespräch (Bearbeitungszeit 20 Minuten)

Situation: Nadine Koch, eine Mitarbeiterin der Personalabteilung eines schottischen Unternehmens in Deutschland, bekommt einen Anruf von Sarah Denby, einer Hochschulabsolventin aus Schottland, die sich um eine Stelle für die Vertriebsabteilung bewirbt.

Aufgabe: Sie hören das Gespräch zweimal. Fassen Sie für den Vertriebsleiter in Deutschland, der über die eingehenden Bewerbungen informiert sein möchte, die wichtigsten Informationen in einem Memo zusammen.

Nadine Koch: Hello, Human Resources, Nadine Koch speaking. What can I do for you?

…

Nadine Koch: Oh yes. Could you just repeat your name, please?

…

Nadine Koch: OK. Mmh. You don't mind my taking notes, Sarah, do you?

…

Nadine Koch: And could I have your address, please?

…

Nadine Koch: If you don't mind …

…

Nadine Koch: I repeat. Your address is 25 Burns Drive, Aberdeen. And your phone number is 01224 for the area and then 286437. And then your mobile phone: 0169-8473621.

…

Nadine Koch: That's fine then. OK Sarah, now tell me something about yourself, your qualifications and your experience.

…

Nadine Koch: Sounds good. Hope that all goes well. And your Highers subjects?

...

Nadine Koch: Any languages, Sarah? How about German?

...

Nadine Koch: And have you got any work experience, done a placement perhaps?

...

Nadine Koch: That sounds absolutely fine. Why don't you send us your CV and then we'll see how it goes from there?

...

Nadine Koch: Well, I'll send you a questionnaire to fill in and you can send that back with all the usual documents to the address on the questionnaire. OK?

...

4
Vermerk in Deutsch über einen in der Fremdsprache abgefassten Geschäftsbrief
(Bearbeitungszeit 30 Minuten)

Situation: Die Ferber Möbel GmbH & Co KG aus Köln hat in Richmond bei London neue Ausstellungsräume für ihre Küchenmöbelausstellung angemietet. Die Räumlichkeiten sollten komplett renoviert werden. Ein Anbieter schickt nachstehendes Schreiben.

Aufgabe: Als Mitarbeiter/in der Geschäftsleitung erstellen Sie einen Vermerk über den Inhalt dieses Briefes in deutscher Sprache.

TOMLINSON REFURBISHING SPECIALISTS LTD
25 Fetcham Road   Leatherhead KT23 4WA

Ferber Möbel GmbH & Co KG
Marconistr 96
50769 Köln

Attn. Mr Simons

Refurbishing of showrooms in Richmond

Dear Mr Simons

Thank you for your enquiry about the reflooring and redecorating work in your Richmond showrooms. In the meantime, I have been able to inspect the showrooms and also to assess the work that needs to be done. My quotation, which you will find enclosed, is made on the basis of close on-site inspection and discussions with Mr Davies, your agent for the London region.

You will note that my quotation does not include the cost of flooring material, wallpaper and curtain materials. This will have to be calculated separately, and the costs very much depend on the type and quality of the materials that you select. Please note that there is a surcharge for additional workmanship on some materials. As soon as you have decided which materials you want us to use in your showrooms, we can furnish a much more detailed and accurate quotation which could then be used as a basis for the award of contract.

I have dispatched a couple of pattern books today for you to select the materials.

We would be in a position to carry out the work within 10 working days after the award of contract and reckon to be able to complete the work within two to three weeks.

If there are any further queries, please do not hesitate to contact us. I hope that you will find our quotation acceptable and look forward to hearing from you again in the near future.

Yours sincerely

Sam Tomlinson

5

Spracherergänzungstest
(Bearbeitungszeit 25 Minuten für beide Texte zusammen)

Text 1
Bitte setzen Sie 20 der 23 angegebenen Wörter oder Wendungen in die Lücken des nachstehenden Textes ein.

> advantageous | amicable | at short notice
> brochure | business relations | business terms
> complaints | convenient | delay in payment
> dispatch | distribution depots | documentary
> enterprise | contact | eventuality | in a position
> invoice | offer | on a large scale | purchasing
> service | to your specifications | umbrellas

Dear Madam, dear Sir

Our local Chamber of Commerce here in Shanghai has informed us that your company is one of the leading German suppliers of large [1] _____ for promotional purposes, and that, as a leading buying agent, we should get in contact with you.

Our [2] _____ has grown substantially over the last ten years. With [3] _____ centres throughout China, we are in [4] _____ with all major manufacturers here. Furthermore, we have also set up several [5] _____ in mainland Europe and Britain. We are, therefore, [6] _____ to buy all types of promotional umbrellas, both plain and imprinted [7] _____, at very [8] _____ prices and dispatch them to customers [9] _____.

Our usual [10] _____ are documents against payment or payment by [11] _____ letter of credit. These terms are [12] _____ to start with, but we would, of course, be willing to negotiate once we have established [13] _____ and are doing business with you [14] _____.

Although we have, as yet, had no [15] _____ about the goods we have supplied or our [16] _____, it is only reasonable to guard against such an [17] _____. We would, therefore, suggest submitting any dispute to your Chamber of Commerce for arbitration, if all attempts at reaching an [18] _____ solution have failed.

We would be very pleased if you made use of our [19] _____ to act as your buying agent here in China. We are, of course, quite prepared to answer any queries you might have. For your information, we have enclosed a [20] _____ about our company and the services we can provide.

Please contact the Hong Kong and Shanghai Banking corporation here in Shanghai for references.

We hope that our offer will be of interest to you and look forward to hearing from you soon.

Yours faithfully

Text 2

In diesem Text ist jeweils nur eine der drei in der Anlage vorgeschlagenen Formen korrekt. Bitte setzen Sie die richtige Lösung in die Lücke ein.

There is a 25 per cent chance that, by the end of today, you will have told at least one [1] _____ lie. Maybe you [2] _____ one already. And what [3] _____ wrong with that? [4] _____ is not so bad, apparently. In [5] _____ of students, about four in five thought it was [6] _____ to lie in a job interview. Nine out of ten said [7] _____ acceptable to lie on a first date. A professor of [8] _____ found that in certain situations lying [9] _____ the liar an advantage over the person being lied to.

Lying cannot be [10] _____ from our social contacts. We learn to lie [11] _____, when we discover the differences between [12] _____ and other people and begin to realise that they have [13] _____ own point of view. We also begin to understand that we can [14] _____ them by [15] _____ or not giving the correct information. Lies [16] _____ as almost positive when they [17] _____ difficult social situations or [18] _____ the ties between people. When someone asks [19] _____ they [20] _____ in an outfit, [21] _____ for a [22] _____ answer. What they [23] _____ has nothing to with the [24] _____ themselves and everything to do with [25] _____ on a social level. Women are considered better at these 'white lies' [26] _____ as they are more aware of the social aspects of what they do or say.

The problem is that the other party may discover the [27] _____ and then people get angry because they realise you were trying to [28] '_____'. Cultural attitudes vary. In Germany, telling the truth is considered correct, even if it [29] _____ nice for the listener. White lies such as saying "Yes, That's a lovely dress" are less [30] _____ than elsewhere in Europe. In other cultures, lies can be acceptable depending on the circumstances.

[1] important
    relevant
    significant

[2] are telling
    had told
    have told

[3] has been
    will be
    would be

[4] laying
    lieing
    lying

[5] a current survey
    a latest survey
    a recent survey

[6] alright
    allright
    alrite

[7] it is
    it will be
    it was

[8] psichology
    psychology
    sychology

[9] gave
    will give
    would give

[10] separate
     separated
     seperated

[11] at about three years old
     at about three year's old
     at about three years' old

[12] ourselfs
     ourselves
     us

[13] our
     their
     there

[14] deceipt
     deceive
     decieve

[15] holding back an information
     holding back information
     holding back informations

[16] may be see
     may even be seen
     may even have seen

[17] smooth above
     smooth over
     smooth under

[18] strengthen
     strength
     stronger

[19] weather
     wether
     whether

[20] look good
     look goodly
     look well

[21] they do not necessarily ask
     they are not necessarily asking
     did not necessarily ask

[22] trusting
     truthful
     truthworthy

[23] are asking for
     have been asking
     have asked for

[24] clothes
     clothing
     cloths

[25] assurance
     insurance
     reassurance

[26] than man
     than men
     then man

[27] intruth
     nontruth
     untruth

[28] cheat
     cheet
     cheeting

[29] may not be
     ought not to be
     will not be

[30] common
     current
     popular

Deutsch – englisches Glossar

Eine Auswahl der wichtigsten Wörter und Begriffe für die Handelskorrespondenz

A

abhängen von	to depend on
Abitur	A-levels [GB]
Abrechnung, vierteljährliche ~	quarterly statement
(Abschluss)Examen machen in	to graduate in
Absender	consignor, shipper, sender
Abweichung	discrepancy
Akkreditiv, unwiderrufliches und bestätiges ~	irrevocable and confirmed letter of credit
Akte	record
anbei	enclosed
Anforderungen entsprechen, unseren ~	to fulfil/meet our requirements
Anfrage	enquiry
angeben, Anschrift / eine Referenz ~	to supply an address / a reference
angeben, einen Preis ~	to quote a price
Angebot	offer
Angebot, günstiges ~	competitive offer
Angebot, (Preis)~	quotation
Angebotsbedingungen	terms of the offer
Angelegenheit mit jdm. besprechen	to take a matter up with s.o.
Anlage	enclosure
annehmen, eine Einladung ~	to accept an invitation
Ansicht, zur	for inspection
Anwalt, (Rechts)~, Anwältin	solicitor
Anzeige	advertisement
aufschieben	to postpone
Auftrag, im ~ von	for/on behalf of
Auftragsausführung	execution of order
Auftragsbearbeitung	order handling/processing
Auftragsbestätigung	acknowledgement/confirmation of (an) order
Auftragsformular	order form
Auftragsnummer	order number
Ausbildung, (Berufs)~	(vocational) training
Ausfuhr	export
ausführen, Auftrag ~	to process/execute an order
Ausgabe	edition, issue
Ausgleich (für), als/zum ~	by way of compensation (for)
ausgleichen, Konto ~	to clear an account
ausliefern	to dispatch, to make delivery
ausmachen, einen Termin ~	to arrange a date
ausnahmsweise	by way of exception
ausschlagen	to line *(Kiste)*
Ausstellungszwecke, für ~	for display purposes
austauschen, Waren ~	to replace goods
auswerten	to evaluate
Auszubildende/r in einem gewerblichen Beruf	apprentice
Auszubildende/r in einem kaufmännischen Beruf	trainee

B

Bahn, per ~	by rail
bald	in due course
Barzahlungsrabatt	cash discount
basieren, auf etw. ~	to be based on
beachtet werden, nicht ~	to go unnoticed
Beamer	video projector
beanstanden, Rechnung ~	to query an invoice
Bedingung, unter der ~, dass	provided that
Bedingungen	conditions
Bedingungen/Konditionen, verbesserte ~	revised terms
Bedürfnissen entsprechen (jds.)	to meet s.o.'s requirements
beeinflussen, etw. nicht ~ können	to be beyond so.'s control
Begleichung, (Rechnung)~	settlement (of invoice)
beiliegend	enclosed
belasten	to debit
Belastungsanzeige	debit note
berechnen	to charge
bereinigen, Fehler ~	to adjust a mistake
bereinigen, eine Sache ~	to put a matter right
bereit sein, etw. zu tun	to be willing
berichtigen	to revise
berichtigen, Rechnung ~	to amend an invoice
beschädigt	damaged
Beschaffung	purchasing
beschäftigt sein	to be tied up
Bescheid, jdm. ~ sagen	to let so. know
Beschwerde	complaint
beschweren, sich ~ über	to complain about
Bestand, ausreichender (Waren)~	adequate stock levels
bestätigen, eine Reservierung ~	to confirm a hotel reservation

bestätigen, einen Termin ~	to confirm an appointment
Betrag, fälliger/offener ~	amount due/owing, outstanding sum/amount
bevorstehend	forthcoming
bewerben, sich um eine (freie) Stelle~	to apply for a job/vacancy/post
Bewerbung	application
Bezahlung bei Bestellung	cash with order (CWO)
Bezug, in ~ auf	further to
Bezug, mit ~ auf	with reference to
Bezugszeichen	reference
Bildungsabschluss, (Berufs)~	(vocational) qualification
Broschüre	brochure
Brutto(preis)	gross (price)

D

dankbar sein	to be grateful
Datenblatt, technisches ~	technical data sheet
Datum, ein ~ festlegen	to fix a date
Doppelzimmer	double room
dringend	urgent
dringend, etw. ~ brauchen	to be desperate for
Dringlichkeit	urgency
Druck, jdn. unter ~ setzen	to put so. under pressure
Durchschlag	carbon copy, copy circulated

E

EDV-Kenntnisse	IT (information technology) skills, computer literacy
EDV-Kenntnisse, über ~ verfügen	to be computer-literate
Eilboten, durch ~	by express, special delivery
Einführungsangebot	introductory offer
Einführungsrabatt	introductory discount
einhalten, genau ~	to strictly adhere to
Einkauf	purchasing
Einkaufsführer	buyer's guide
Einkaufsleiter/in	purchasing manager
einladen	to invite
Einladung	invitation
Einschreiben	registered mail
Einzelzimmer	single room
Einzelhandelsgeschäft	retail outlet
Einzelheiten	details
Empfänger/in	addressee
empfehlen	to recommend
Empfehlung	recommendation
Empfehlungsschreiben	testimonial, reference
Entschädigung	compensation
entschuldigen, sich ~	to apologise
Erfahrung, (Berufs)~	(work) experience
Erfahrungen machen/sammeln	to gain experience
erfüllen, jds. Erwartungen ~	to meet one's expectations
Ergänzung	amendment (*Vertrag*)
Erhalt, innerhalb 14 Tagen nach ~ von	within a fortnight of receipt of
Ermäßigung anbieten	to offer a reduction
Ersatz(stück)	replacement
Ersatzsendung/-lieferung	replacement consignment/supply
Erstauftrag	initial order
erweitern, (Sortiment) ~	to extend (a range)

F

Fabrik	plant
Fehler in der Rechnungsstellung	accounting error
Fertigkeiten	skills
festlegen	to stipulate
festlegen, endgültig ~	to finalise
Filiale	branch
Firmenname, eingetragener ~	registered name
Folgeauftrag	follow-up order
Frachtführer	carrier
Frachtraum	shipping space
frei Haus	franco domicile
freibleibend	subject to confirmation
Freiumschlag, adressierter ~	self-addressed / stamp-addressed envelope
Frist für die (Rechnungs) Begleichung	deadline for payment
führend	leading
Füllmaterial	padding material

G

Garantie	warranty, guarantee
Garantiefrist	period of guarantee
garantieren	to guarantee
geeignet	suitable
Gefallen, einen ~ tun	to be obliged
Gegenangebot	counteroffer
Gelegenheit nutzen, die ~	to take the opportunity
gemäß	as per
gemäß, (dem Gesetz) ~	compliance with (the law)
gemeinsam(er Kunde)	mutual (customer)
genau	accurate
genehmigen	to authorise
Geschäfte mit jdm. machen	to do business with so.
Geschäftsangelegenheiten	business matters
Geschäftsbedingungen, (allgemeine) ~	(general) terms and conditions of business
Geschäftsbeziehung	business relationship
Geschäftsräume	premises
Geschäftsstelle	branch
Geschäftsverkehr	business dealings
gewährleisten	to ensure
Gewährleistung	warranty, guarantee
Großauftrag	bulk/volume order

Großhandel	wholesale
Groß- und Außenhandelskaufmann/-frau	Management Assistant in Wholesale and Foreign Trade
Großhändler	wholesaler
gültig	valid
günstig	advantageous
gut eingeführt	well-established
Güter	goods
Güterspedition	(road) haulier, haulage company
gutschreiben	to credit
Gutschriftanzeige	credit note

H

Handelskammer, (Industrie- und) ~	chamber of commerce
Handelsrabatt	trade discount
Händen, zu ~ von	for the attention of
Handhabung	handling
herstellen	to manufacture
Hersteller/in	manufacturer
Hochachtungsvoll	Yours faithfully
hochwertig	top-quality

I

Importeur	importer
Informationen liefern	to supply information
informieren, jdn. ~	to advise/inform sb.
interessieren, sich ~ für	to be interested in

K

Katalog	catalogue
Kaufvertrag	contract of sale
Kette	chain
Klage (vor Gericht)	legal action
klären	to clarify
klein gedruckt	in small print
Kommission, in ~	on sale or return
Konferenzraum	conference room
kontaktieren, jdn. ~	to get in touch with so., to contact so.
Kontoaufstellung	(account) statement
Kontoauszug	(account) statement
Kosten, auf Ihre ~	at your expense
Kunde/Kundin	customer
Kundenangaben, nach ~ hergestellt/gefertigt	custom-made/customised
Kundenangaben, nach ~ herstellen/anfertigen	to make to customer's specifications

L

Ladung	shipment, consignment
Lager	stores
Lager, ab ~ liefern	to supply from stock
Lebenslauf	CV (curriculum vitae), résumé, personal data sheet (PDS)
Lehre (gewerblich)	apprenticeship
Lehre (kaufmännisch)	traineeship
Liefer- und Zahlungsbedingungen	terms of payment and delivery
Lieferant	supplier
Lieferbedingungen	delivery terms, terms of delivery
Lieferfrist	delivery period
liefern	to supply
Lieferplan	delivery schedule
Lieferschein	delivery/dispatch note
Liefertermin	delivery date
Liefertermin nennen	to quote a delivery date
Lieferung	delivery; shipment/consignment
Lieferung und Transport, kostenlose ~	free delivery and transport
Lieferung, verspätete ~	late delivery
Lieferungs(bedürfnisse)	delivery (requirements)
Lieferverpflichtungen	delivery commitments
Liefervertrag	supply contract
Lieferverzug	delay in delivery
Listenpreis, unter ~	below list (price)
LKW, per ~	by road
Luftfracht, per ~	by air
Luftpost, mit ~	by air mail

M

Mahnschreiben	reminder, collection letter
Mandant/in	principal
Mängelrüge	complaint
Marketing	marketing
Marketingleiter/in	marketing manager
Markt	market
Markt bringen, etw. auf den ~	to launch
melden (sich bei jdm.)	to get in touch with so., to contact so.
Mengenrabatt	volume discount
Messe	(trade) fair
(Messe)Stand	stand (at a trade fair)
minderwertig	substandard, inferior
Minusbetrag	debit balance
Mit besten Grüßen	Best wishes
Mit freundlichen Grüßen	Yours sincerely
mitteilen, Anschrift / Referenz ~	to supply an address / a reference
Modellnummer	model number
möglich, wenn ~	if possible
Muster	sample, specimen

N

Nachbestellung	repeat order
nachkommen, seinen (Zahlungs) Verpflichtungen	to meet one's (financial) obligations/commitments
Nachlass anbieten	to offer a reduction
Nachnahme, per ~	payment on delivery (P/D)
nachsenden	to forward
nennen, einen Preis ~	to quote a price
Netto(preis)	net (price)

P

packen, voll ~	to pack
Packliste	packing list
Paletten verpacken, auf ~	to palletise
Partie	batch, shipment, consignment
passend	suitable
passt, wie es Ihnen ~	at your convenience
Post, mit getrennter ~	by separate post, under separate cover
Postleitzahl	post code, ZIP code
Praktikum (machen)	(to do an) internship, a placement
präsentieren	to demonstrate, to present
Preise, wettbewerbsfähige ~	competitive prices
Preisliste	price list
Probe(stück)	sample, specimen
Probeauftrag	trial order
Probezwecke, zu ~	for testing purposes
Produktionsumfang	production volume
Produktreihe	product line
Prospekt	brochure, leaflet
Prospektmaterial	sales material/literature
Prüfung	examination

Q

Quartalsabrechnung	quarterly statement

R

Rabatt	discount
Rabatte/Preise, neue ~	revised discounts/prices
Rechnung	invoice
Rechnung, in ~ stellen	to charge
Rechnung bezahlen/begleichen	to settle an invoice
Rechnungsbegleichung	settlement of an invoice
Rechnungswesen	accounting
Referenz	reference
Registernummer	registration number
Reihe, genau der ~ nach	on a strict rota basis
Reisepläne	travel arrangements/plans
reklamieren, Rechnung ~	to query an invoice
reservieren lassen, ein Zimmer im Hotel ~	to make a hotel reservation
Restbetrag	remainder/remaining amount/sum, balance
richten, sich ~ nach	to conform to
Rückgaberecht, mit ~	on sale or return

S

schaffen, sich an etw. zu ~ machen	to tamper with s.th.
schuld sein	to be s.o.'s fault
Seefracht, per ~	by sea
Sekretär/in	secretary/PA (personal assistant)
Sehr geehrte Damen und Herren	Dear Sir or Madam
Sendung	batch, shipment, consignment
Sicherheitsregeln	safety regulations
Skonto	cash discount
Sonderbedingungen	special terms
Sortiment	range
Spediteur	forwarding/shipping agent, freight forwarder
Spedition	carrier
Spedition(sfirma)	shipper
Sprachkenntnisse, gute ~	good command of a language
Standardprodukt	off-the-shelf product
Stellenbewerbung	job application
Steuer	tax
stornieren, Auftrag ~	to cancel an order
Straßenspediteur	(road) haulier, haulage company
Sommerkollektion	summer collection

T

Tageslichtprojektor	overhead projector
Tagesordnung	agenda
Tagungsmöglichkeiten	conference facilities
Teilzahlung	part/partial payment
Transportfirma	carrier
Transportmittel	means of transport
Transportvereinbarungen	transport arrangements
Transportweg, auf dem ~	in transit
Tunnelterminal	tunnel terminal

U

übereinstimmen mit	to tally with
überfällig sein	to be overdue
übersehen	to overlook
überweisen	to transfer, to remit
Überweisung	remittance, transfer
Unannehmlichkeiten, jdm. ~ bereiten	to inconvenience s.o.
ungünstig	inconvenient
Unstimmigkeit	discrepancy

Unterlagen, für unsere ~	for our files
unterschreiben	to sign
Unterschriften	signature block
untersuchen	to examine
untersuchen, Angelegenheit ~	to investigate / look into a matter
Untersuchung	examination
unterwegs	in transit
Unterzeichner	undersigned
unverbindlich	subject to confirmation
unzufrieden sein über	to be dissatisfied with

V

verändern	to revise
veranlassen, Lieferung ~	to arrange for delivery to be made
verantwortlich sein	to be to blame
Verantwortung übernehmen für	to accept responsibility for
Verarbeitung	finish, workmanship
verbindlich	binding/firm
Verbindung, in ~ bringen mit	to relate to
vereinbaren	to arrange
vereinbaren, einen Termin ~	to make an appointment
vereinbart, es gilt als ~	it is agreed
vereinbart, wie	as agreed
Verfügung, zu jds. ~ bereithalten	to hold at s.o.'s disposal
verhandeln	to negotiate
Verkaufsstelle	outlet
verkratzt	scratched
Verlängerung des Zahlungsziels gewähren	to grant an extension
verlegen, Termin ~	to postpone an appointment
Verlust(e), jds. ~ decken	to cover s.o.'s losses
Verpackung	packing, packaging
Verpackung, schadhafte/beschädigte ~	defective packing
Verpflichtung, eine andere ~	prior engagement
Versandanweisungen	instructions for shipment/dispatch
Versandanzeige	advice of dispatch/shipment, delivery/advice note
versandfertig, versandbereit	ready for dispatch/shipment
versenden	to ship
Versender	consignor, shipper
Versicherung	insurance
Vertreter/in, (Handels)~	agent
Vertrieb	distribution
Vertrieb(sgesellschaft)	distributor
Verzögerung in der (Aus)Lieferung	delay in delivery
vorbehalten, sich das Recht ~	to reserve the right
vorlegen	to submit
vorrätig sein	to be in stock
vorrätig, nicht (mehr) ~ sein	to be out of stock
vorschlagen, ein Datum ~	to suggest a date
Vorstellungsgespräch	(job) interview
Vorstellungsgespräch mit jdm. führen	to interview s.o.
Vorstellungsgespräch, jdn. zum ~ einladen	to invite s.o. for an interview
vorteilhaft	advantageous

W

Ware	goods
Waren bezeichnen	to identify goods
Waren, fehlerhafte ~	faulty goods
was ... betrifft/angeht	as far as ... goes / is concerned
Weitertransport	forward carriage / on-carriage
Werbung machen	to advertise
Werk	plant
Wettbewerbslage	competitive situation
Woche, in der ~ vom ...	in the week commencing ...

Z

Zahlungs-/Geschäftsbedingungen	terms of payment/business
Zahlungsaufforderung	request for payment
Zahlungsaufschub	delayed payment terms
Zahlungserinnerung	reminder, collection letter
Zahlungsfrist	time allowed for payment
Zahlungsfrist überschreiten / nicht beachten	to exceed a credit period
Zahlungsverzug	delay in payment
Zahlungsziel, langfristiges	extended credit terms, long-term credit
Zeit, zu gegebener ~	in due course
zerrissen	torn
Zeugnis	certificate
zufrieden stellend	satisfactory
zukommen lassen, jdm. etw. ~	to provide so. with
Zurück, falls unzustellbar	return if undelivered
zurückstellen	to postpone
zurückweisen, Reklamation/Beschwerde ~	to reject a complaint/claim
Zusatz-	additional
Zuschlag	surcharge
Zustand, in gutem ~	in good order and condition
zwischenzeitlich	meanwhile

Wörterverzeichnis A–Z

Diese Liste enthält alle Wörter in alphabetischer Reihenfolge. Hier sind jedoch die Wörter, die zum Grundwortschatz gehören, sowie internationale Wörter wie *fax*, *hotel* oder *job* nicht aufgeführt. Die Zahl nach dem Stichwort bezieht sich auf die Seite, auf der das Wort zum ersten Mal erscheint.

T = das Wort befindet sich in den *Transcripts* zu der *Listening*-Übung auf der betreffenden Seite.

A

abbreviation 8 *Abkürzung*
to accept responsibility for 98 *Verantwortung übernehmen für*
acceptance, upon firm ~ 56 *nach verbindlicher Zusage*
accounts 112 *Buchhaltung(sabteilung)*
accurate 4 *genau*
acknowledgement 58 *Auftragsbestätigung*
additional 43 *Zusatz-*
to address 6 *adressieren*
address, inside ~ 6 *Empfängeranschrift*
addressee 4 *Adressat/in, Empfänger/in*
adhere, to strictly ~ to 76 *genau einhalten*
to adjust 65 *korrigieren, anpassen*
advantageous 68 *günstig, vorteilhaft*
to advertise 6 *Werbung machen*
advertisement 5 *Anzeige*
advice note 81 *Versandanzeige*
advice of dispatch/shipment 81 *Versandanzeige*
to advise 70 *informieren, in Kenntnis setzen*
agenda 26 *Tagesordnung*
agent 38 *(Handels)Vertreter/in, Vermittler/in*
agreed, as ~ 56 *wie vereinbart, verabredungsgemäß*
agreed, it is ~ 79 *es gilt als vereinbart*
air, by ~ 50 *per Luftfracht*
air mail, by ~ 13 *mit Luftpost*
A-levels 109 *(entspricht) Abitur*
to amend an invoice 93 *Rechnung berichtigen*
amendment (Vertrag) 60 *Ergänzung*
amount due 83 *fälliger/offener Betrag*
amount owing 93 *fälliger/offener Betrag*
amount, outstanding ~ 93 *fälliger/offener Betrag*
amount, remaining ~ 93 *Restbetrag*
to apologise 94 *sich entschuldigen*
to apply for a job/vacancy 106 *sich um eine (freie) Stelle bewerben*
to apply for a post 117 *sich um eine (freie) Stelle bewerben*
appointment, to arrange an ~ 14 *einen Termin abmachen*
appointment, to confirm an ~ 25 *einen Termin bestätigen*
appointment, to make an ~ 25 *einen Termin vereinbaren*
appointment, to postpone an ~ 36 *einen Termin verlegen*
apprentice(ship) 117 *Lehrling (Lehre) in einem gewerblichen Beruf*
to arrange 25 *vereinbaren, ausmachen*
to arrange for delivery to be made 59 *die Lieferung veranlassen*
as far as ... goes / is concerned 26 *was ... betrifft/angeht*
to attach 66 *beilegen*
to attend 33 *teilnehmen an*
attend, to ~ a course 115 *einen Kurs besuchen*
attention, for the ~ of 31 *zu Händen von*
attention, will have our immediate ~ 63 *wird umgehend bearbeitet*
to authorise 60 *genehmigen, zustimmen zu*
Automobile Sales Management Assistant 107 *Automobilkaufmann/-frau*
available, to be ~ 14 *erreichbar sein*
aware, to be ~ of sth 96 *sich einer Sache bewusst sein*

B

background information 37 *Hintergrundinformationen*
balance, (debit) ~ 86 *(Minusbetrag), Restbetrag*
Bank Business Management Assistant 107 *Bankkaufmann/-frau*
based in 46 *ansässig in*
to be based on 35 *auf etw. basieren*
batch 34 *Sendung, Partie*
behalf, for/on ~ of 10 *im Auftrag von*
binding 51 *verbindlich*
blame, to be to ~ 94 *verantwortlich/schuld sein*
body of letter 6 *Brieftext*
branch 31 *Filiale, Geschäftsstelle*
to break 27 *zerbrechen*
breakage 27 *Bruch*
brief, to be ~ 4 *um es kurz zu machen*
broadcaster 21 *Rundfunk-/Fernsehanstalt*
brochure 5 *Prospekt, Broschüre*
bulk order 43 *Großauftrag*
business management 109 *Betriebswirtschaft(slehre)*
business matters 4 *Geschäftsangelegenheiten*
business relationship 94 *Geschäftsbeziehung*
business with s.o., to do ~ 46 *Geschäfte mit jdm. machen*
button 43 *Knopf*
buyer's guide 37 *Einkaufsführer*

C

cable connectors 46 *Kabelanschlüsse*
camping equipment 54 *Campingausrüstung*
to cancel an order 58 *einen Auftrag stornieren*
to cancel out 88 *aufheben, zunichte machen*
candidate 114 T *Kandidat/in*
canteen 27 *Kantine*
capacity, in the ~ of a(n) 113 *in der Eigenschaft einer/s*
carbon copy 5 *Durchschlag*
carrier 74 *Transportfirma, Spedition, Frachtführer*
cash discount 48 *Skonto, Barzahlungsrabatt*
cash with order (CWO) 50 *Bezahlung bei Bestellung*
catalogue 5 *Katalog*
category 21 *Kategorie*
caution marks 77 *Markierungen*
certificate 106 *Bescheinigung; hier: Zeugnis*
certificate, school-leaving ~ 109 *Abschlusszeugnis*
chain 45 *Kette*
chamber of commerce 37 *Handelskammer*
to charge 93 *in Rechnung stellen, berechnen*
china 99 *Porzellan*
to clarify 69 *klären*
to clear an account 83 *Konto ausgleichen*

collection letter 82 *Zahlungserinnerung, Mahnschreiben*
collection, summer ~ 38 *Sommerkollektion*
command of a language, good ~ 108 *gute Sprachkenntnisse*
commitments, to meet one's (financial) ~ 85 *seinen (Zahlungs)Verpflichtungen nachkommen*
communicative skills 116 *Kommunikationsfähigkeit, -kompetenz*
community service 109 *Zivildienst*
compensation 98 *Entschädigung*
compensation, by way of ~ (for) 105 *als/zum Ausgleich (für)*
competitive 46 *konkurrenzfähig*
competitive offer 40 *günstiges Angebot*
competitive prices 65 *wettbewerbsfähige Preise*
competitive situation 68 *Wettbewerbslage*
to complain about 95 *sich beschweren über*
complaint 34 *Beschwerde, Mängelrüge*
complaint, to make a ~ 94 *sich beschweren, etwas reklamieren*
compliance with 46 *Erfüllung*
complimentary close 6 *höfliche Schlussformel*
computer literacy 109 *EDV-Kenntnisse*
conditions 48 *Bedingungen*
conference centre 16 T *Konferenzzentrum*
conference facilities 28 *Tagungsmöglichkeiten*
conference room 31 *Konferenzraum*
confident 102 *zuversichtlich*
confirmation of (an) order 65 *Auftragsbestätigung*
to conform to 46 *sich richten nach*
to consider 33 *erwägen*
considerable 88 *erheblich*
consignment 50 *Sendung, Ladung, Lieferung, Partie*
construction site 77 T *Baustelle*
consultancy 14 *Beratung*
to contact s.o. 33 *sich bei jdm. melden*
contemporary 43 *gegenwärtig*
content 52 *zufrieden*
contract of sale 68 *Kaufvertrag*
control, to be beyond s.o.'s ~ 85 *etw. nicht beeinflussen können*
convenient 33 *günstig, passend*
conversational 4 *Unterhaltungs-, locker*
to copy 7 *abschreiben*
copy circulated 5 *Durchschlag*
corduroy 95 *Kord(samt)*
counteroffer 57 *Gegenangebot*
countless 14 *zahllos*
course, in due ~ 42 *zu gegebener Zeit, bald*
to cover s.o.'s losses 98 *jds. Verlust(e) decken*
cover(ing) letter 106 *Bewerbungsschreiben*
cover, under separate ~ 13 *mit getrennter Post*
to credit 88 *gutschreiben*
current 37 *aktuell*
customer 32 *Kunde/Kundin*
customised 69 *nach Kundenangaben hergestellt/gefertigt*
custom-made 81 *nach Kundenangaben hergestellt/gefertigt*
CV (curriculum vitae) 106 *Lebenslauf*

D

damaged 97 *beschädigt*
data sheet, technical ~ 46 *technisches Datenblatt*
deadline for payment 82 *Zahlungsfrist*
to deal with 25 *verhandeln mit*
to deal with a matter 66 *eine Anlegenheit bearbeiten*

to debit 93 *belasten*
degree course 108 *Studiengang*
delay in delivery 69 *Lieferverzug*
delivery 12 *Liste, Übersicht*
delivery (requirements) 37 *Lieferung(serfordernisse)*
delivery commitments 81 *Lieferverpflichtungen*
delivery date 69 *Liefertermin*
delivery note 81 *Lieferschein, Versandanzeige*
delivery period 69 *Lieferfrist*
delivery schedule 26 *Lieferplan*
delivery terms 58 *Lieferbedingungen*
delivery, free ~ and transport 49 *kostenlose Lieferung und Transport*
delivery, late ~ 75 *verspätete Lieferung*
delivery, to make ~ 72 *(aus)liefern*
demand 78 *Nachfrage*
to demonstrate 30 *präsentieren*
denim 38 *Jeansstoff*
to depend on 53 *abhängen von*
depending on 48 *je nach*
deputy 112 *Vertretungs-*
desk, (patented) high ~ 45 *(patentiertes) Stehpult*
desperate, to be ~ for 44 *etw. dringend brauchen*
details 12 *Einzelheiten*
to dictate 21 *diktieren*
disappointed (about) 100 *enttäuscht (über)*
disappointment 96 *Enttäuschung*
discount 27 *Rabatt*
discrepancy 82 *Abweichung, Unstimmigkeit*
dispatch 54 *Lieferung*
dispatch, ready for ~ 60 *versandfertig, versandbereit*
to dispatch 50 *ausliefern*
dispatch note 81 *Lieferschein*
display space 45 *Austellungsfläche*
disposal, to hold at s.o.'s ~ 95 *zu jds. Verfügung bereithalten*
to disregard 83 *ignorieren, nicht beachten*
dissatisfied with 105 *unzufrieden über*
distribution 52 *Vertrieb*
distributor 5 *Vertrieb(sgesellschaft)*
domestic market 68 *heimischer Markt; Binnenmarkt*
double room 36 *Doppelzimmer*
draft for acceptance 80 *Tratte nach Annahme*
due to 33 *aufgrund*

E

eager 43 *begierig, erwartungsvoll*
edition 5 *Ausgabe*
electrical garden equipment 46 *Elektrogartengeräte*
electronic parts 67 *Elektronik-Zubehörteile*
embassy 14 *Botschaft*
enclosed 5 *anbei, beiliegend*
enclosure 5 *Anlage*
engaged 24 *besetzt*
engagement, prior ~ 31 *eine andere Verpflichtung*
enquiry 5 *Anfrage*
ensuite bathroom 28 *Zimmer mit Bad*
to ensure 81 *sicher stellen, gewährleisten*
entirely 54 *vollkommen*
envelope, self-addressed / stamp-addressed ~ 13 *adressierter Freiumschlag*
envelope, window ~ 7 *Fensterumschlag*

to envisage 33 hier: *vorhaben*
error, accounting ~ 82 *Fehler in der Rechnungsstellung*
essentially 33 *im Wesentlichen*
to evaluate 39 *auswerten, beurteilen*
to exaggerate 14 *übertreiben*
examination 105 *Untersuchung, Prüfung*
to examine 39 *untersuchen, prüfen*
to exceed a credit period 85 *Zahlungsfrist überschreiten*
except for 78 *außer*
exception, by way of ~ 96 *ausnahmsweise*
excess, in ~ of 52 *über, höher als*
to execute an order 68 *Auftrag ausführen*
exhibition, furniture ~ 45 *Möbelaustellung*
exhibition ground 16 T *Messegelände*
expectations, to meet one's ~ 97 *jds. Erwartungen erfüllen*
expense, at your ~ 29 *auf Ihre Kosten*
experience, (work) ~ 107 *(Berufs)Erfahrung, (praktische) Erfahrung*
experienced 14 *erfahren*
express, by ~ 13 *durch Eilboten*
to extend (a range) 41 *(Sortiment) erweitern*
extended credit terms 88 *langfristiges Zahlungsziel*
extension number 24 *Durchwahl*

F

failure 88 *Versäumnis*
fair, (trade) ~ 16 T *Messe*
fault, to be s.o.'s ~ 94 *schuld sein*
faulty goods 94 *fehlerhafte Waren*
field representative 113 *Außenvertreter/in*
files, for our ~ 60 *für unsere Unterlagen*
to finalise 33 *endgültig festlegen*
finish 48 *Verarbeitung*
firm 51 *verbindlich*
fitter 112 *Monteur*
to fix a date/time 14 *ein(e) Datum/Zeit festlegen*
follow-up order 64 *Folgeauftrag*
forthcoming 59 *bevorstehend*
to forward 13 *nachsenden*
forward carriage 77 *Weitertransport*
forwarding agent 76 *Spediteur, Spedition*
franco domicile 61 *frei Haus*
free, to be ~ 22 T *erreichbar sein*
free of charge 78 *kostenlos*
freight forwarder 81 *Spedition, Spediteur*
fridge, compact ~ 56 *Elektrokühlbox*
to fulfil our requirements 40 *unseren Anforderungen entsprechen*
full board 36 *Vollpension*
furniture 64 *Möbel*
further to 28 *in Bezug auf*

G

to gain experience 108 *Erfahrungen machen/sammeln*
GCSE 109 *(entspricht) Mittlere Reife*
generosity, to return s.o.'s ~ 29 *jds. Großzügigkeit erwidern*
generous 48 *großzügig*
to get in touch 25 *sich bei jdm. melden*
global economy 14 *Weltwirtschaft*
goods 48 *Güter, Ware*
to grant an extension 87 *Zahlungsaufschub/Verlängerung des Zahlungsziels*
grateful 5 *dankbar*

gross (price) 42 *Brutto(preis)*
guarantee 63 *Gewährleistung, Garantie*
to guarantee 8 *garantieren*
guarantee, period of ~ 98 *Garantiefrist*

H

half board 36 *Halbpension*
handling 72 *Handhabung, Transport*
haulage company 81 *(Straßen)Spediteur, (Güter)Spedition*
haulier, (road) ~ 72 *(Straßen)Spediteur, (Güter)Spedition*
hedge trimmers 46 *Heckenschere*
hesitate, don't ~ to contact me 33 *wenden Sie sich ruhig an mich*
high-quality 46 *hochwertig*
hinge 34 *Scharnier*
to hold the line 15 T *am Apparat bleiben*
home market 68 *heimischer Markt; Binnenmarkt*
human resources 112 *Personal(abteilung)*

I

importer 41 *Importeur*
to include 40 *enthalten*
to inconvenience s.o. 71 *jdm. Unannehmlichkeiten bereiten*
inconvenient 30 *ungelegen, ungünstig*
Industrial Business Management Assistant 107 *Industriekaufmann/-frau*
inferior 68 *minderwertig*
to inform 33 *informieren*
initial order 62 *Erstauftrag*
initials 9 *Initialen*
ink jet printer 54 *Tintenstrahldrucker*
inspection, for ~ 42 *zur Ansicht*
instructions 78 *Anweisungen*
instructions for dispatch 81 *Versandanweisungen*
instructions for shipment 76 *Versandanweisungen*
insurance 34 T *Versicherung*
Insurance Business Management Assistant 107 *Versicherungskaufmann/-frau*
interest 88 *Zinsen*
interested, to be ~ in 5 *sich interessieren für*
internet connection 31 *Internetverbindung*
internship, to do an ~ 107 *ein Praktikum machen*
interview, (job) ~ 107 *Vorstellungsgespräch*
introductory discount 50 *Einführungsrabatt*
introductory offer 52 *Einführungsangebot*
to investigate a matter 101 *Angelegenheit untersuchen*
invitation 25 *Einladung*
invitation, to accept an ~ 29 *eine Einladung annehmen*
to invite 29 *einladen*
invoice 31 *Rechnung*
invoice, pro forma ~ 67 *Pro-forma-Rechnung*
issue 44 *Ausgabe*
IT (information technology) skills 107 *EDV-Kenntnisse*
items, the ~ in question 96 *die betroffenen Artikel*
itinerary 33 *(Reise)Route*

J

jargon 4 *Fachsprache*
job application 106 *Stellenbewerbung*
job change 106 *Stellenwechsel, Wechsel des Arbeitsplatzes*
job training 114 *Ausbildung*
joint owner 14 *Mitbesitzer*

L

to launch 41 *etw. auf den Markt bringen*
leading 5 *führend*
leaflet 41 *Prospekt*
legal action 82 *Klage (vor Gericht)*
to let s.o. know 26 *jdm. Bescheid sagen*
letter of credit, irrevocable and confirmed ~ 51 *unwiderrufliches und bestätiges Akkreditiv*
letterhead 6 *Briefkopf*
likely, to be ~ to 64 *wird wahrscheinlich*
to line *(Kiste)* 77 *ausschlagen*
line, to be on another ~ 24 *auf einer anderen Leitung sprechen*
list (price), below ~ 49 *unter Listenpreis*
long-term credit 88 *langfristiges Zahlungsziel*
to look forward to 5 *sich freuen auf*
to look into a matter 96 *Angelegenheit untersuchen*
low-margin 89 *mit niedriger Gewinnspanne*
luxury 34 T *Luxus-*

M

maintenance 112 *Wartung*
major 66 *groß, größer*
make 44 *Fabrikat*
Management Assistant in Advertising 107 *Werbekaufmann/-frau*
Management Assistant in Event Organisation 107 *Veranstaltungskaufmann/-frau*
Management Assistant in Hotel and Hospitality 107 *Hotelkaufmann/-frau*
Management Assistant in Informatics 107 *Informatikkaufmann/-frau*
Management Assistant in Retail Business 107 *Kaufmann/-frau im Einzelhandel*
Management Assistant in Wholesale and Foreign Trade 107 *Kaufmann/-frau im Groß- und Außenhandel*
manufacturer 5 *Hersteller/in*
maritime 46 *See-*
market 41 *Markt*
to market 14 *verkaufen, vertreiben*
marketing 5 *Marketing*
marketing manager 33 *Marketingleiter/in*
to match 95 *übereinstimmen mit, passen zu*
material, padding ~ 77 *Füllmaterial*
materials, input ~ 79 *Vormaterialen*
matter, to put a ~ right 94 *eine Sache berichtigen/bereinigen*
matter, to take a ~ up with s.o. 103 *eine Angelegenheit mit jdm. besprechen*
means of delivery 48 *Lieferungsmodalitäten*
means of transport 69 *Transportmittel*
meanwhile 60 *zwischenzeitlich*
medium-sized 35 *mittelgroß, mittelständisch*
to meet our requirements 46 *unseren Anforderungen entsprechen*
message, to leave a ~ 14 *eine Nachricht hinterlassen*
message, to take a ~ 15 T *etw. ausrichten*
microfiltration plant 56 *Mikrofilteranlagen*
mileage 34 T *Meilenstand*
to mislead 96 *täuschen*
mix-up 90 T *Durcheinander*
model number 37 *Modellnummer*
to motivate 37 *motivieren*
mutual (customer) 41 *gemeinsam(er Kunde)*

N

name, registered ~ 7 *eingetragener Firmenname*
to negotiate 60 *verhandeln*
net (price) 42 *Netto(preis)*
to note 59 *zur Kenntnis nehmen*
number, registration ~ 7 *hier: Steuernummer*
numbers, back ~ 44 *alte Ausgabe*

O

obligations, to meet one's (financial) ~ 85 *seinen (Zahlungs)Verpflichtungen nachkommen*
to be obliged 39 *einen Gefallen tun*
to obtain 43 *bekommen*
to occur 99 *geschehen*
offer 37 *Angebot*
to offer one's apologies 105 *sich entschuldigen*
Office Management Assistant 107 *Bürokaufmann/-frau*
off-the-shelf product 48 *Standardprodukt*
on-carriage 81 *Weitertransport*
opening 31 *Einweihung*
opportunity, to take the ~ 30 *die Gelegenheit nutzen*
order and condition, in good ~ 102 *in gutem Zustand*
order form 58 *Auftragsformular*
order number 37 *Auftragsnummer*
outlet 68 *Verkaufsstelle*
to overdo it 48 *es übertreiben*
to be overdue 83 *überfällig sein*
overhead projector 31 *Tageslichtprojektor*
to overlook 82 *übersehen*

P

to pack 32 *voll packen*
packaging 81 *Verpackung*
packing 69 *Verpackung*
packing, defective ~ 94 *schadhafte/beschädigte Verpackung*
packing list 90 T *Packliste*
to palletise 72 *auf Paletten verpacken*
parking, off-road ~ 28 *Parkmöglichkeiten abseits der Straße*
part/partial payment 87 *Teilzahlung, Zahlung eines Teilbetrags*
part shipment 91 *Teillieferung*
particularly 5 *besonders, insbesondere*
part-time work 109 *Teilzeitarbeit*
payment, delay in ~ 84 *Zahlungsverzug*
payment, time allowed for ~ 82 *Zahlungsfrist*
payment on delivery (P/D) 50 *per Nachnahme*
payment terms, delayed ~ 82 *Zahlungsaufschub*
per, as ~ 72 *gemäß*
personal assistant (PA) 25 *persönliche/r Assistent/in*
personal data sheet (PDS) 106 *Lebenslauf*
to place an order 53 *eine Bestellung aufgeben*
plant 55 *Fabrik, Werk*
plastic 46 *Kunststoff*
point, keep to the ~ 4 *beim Thema bleiben*
polytechnic 108 *Fachhochschule*
possible, if ~ 30 *wenn möglich*
post code 7 *Postleitzahl*
to postpone 95 *zurückstellen, aufschieben*
power station, coal-fired ~ 56 *Kohlekraftwerk*
premises 40 *Geschäftsräume*
to present 30 *präsentieren*

press-stud 43 *Druckknopf*
pressure, to put s.o. under ~ 53 *jdn. unter Druck setzen*
price-list 5 *Preisliste*
principal 77 T *Klient/in, Mandant/in*
to process an order 60 *Auftrag ausführen*
product line 30 *Produktreihe*
production volume 34 *Produktionsumfang*
prompt 35 *Stichpunkt*
to pronounce 15 T *aussprechen*
properly 32 *richtig, gut*
property 52 *Gebäude, Eigentum*
prospect, hold out the ~ of 45 *in Aussicht stellen*
to provide s.o. with 47 *jdm. etw. zukommen lassen*
provided that 56 *unter der Bedingung, dass*
pulse counter 53 T *Impulszähler*
purchasing 5 *Beschaffung, Einkauf*
purchasing manager 6 *Einkaufsleiter/in*
purposes, for display ~ 68 *für Ausstellungszwecke*
to put s.o. through 14 *jdn. durchstellen*

Q

qualification, (vocational) ~ 106 *(Berufs)Bildungsabschluss*
qualifying examination 109 *Ausbildungsabschlussprüfung*
query 43 *Nachfrage*
to query an invoice 90 *eine Rechnung reklamieren/beanstanden*
quotation 37 *(Preis)Angebot*
to quote a delivery date 57 *einen Liefertermin nennen*
to quote a price 40 *einen Preis angeben/nennen*

R

rail, by ~ 50 *per Bahn*
range 5 *Sortiment, Angebot, Produktpalette*
to react to 40 *reagieren auf*
receipt, within a fortnight of ~ 49 *innerhalb von 14 Tagen nach Erhalt*
reception 31 *Empfang*
to recommend 37 *empfehlen*
recommendation 37 *Empfehlung*
record 12 *Akte, Unterlage*
reduction, to offer a ~ 98 *Nachlass/Ermäßigung anbieten*
ref, Our/Your ~: 9 *Unser/Ihr Zeichen*
reference 6; 107 *Bezugszeichen; Referenz, Empfehlungsschreiben*
reference, with ~ to 50 *mit Bezug auf*
regards, with best/kind ~ 10 *Viele Grüße*
registered mail 13 *Einschreiben*
to reject a complaint 94 *Reklamation/Beschwerde zurückweisen*
to relate to 53 *in Verbindung bringen mit*
remainder 78 *Rest(betrag)*
reminder 52 *Mahnung, Zahlungserinnerung, Mahnschreiben*
to remit 93 *überweisen*
remittance 83 *Überweisung*
to repeat 24 *wiederholen*
repeat order 52 *Folgeauftrag*
to replace goods 98 *Waren ersetzen/austauschen*
replacement 94 *Ersatz(stück)*
replacement supply 94 *Ersatzsendung/Ersatzlieferung*
representative 30 *Außendienstmitarbeiter/in*
request 40 *Bitte*
request for payment 82 *Zahlungsaufforderung*
requirement, absolute ~ 46 *unabdingbare Voraussetzung*
requirements, in line with market ~ 45 *marktgerecht*
requirements, to meet all ~ 56 *alle Anforderungen erfüllen*

reservation, to confirm a hotel ~ 25 *eine Reservierung bestätigen*
reservation, to make a hotel ~ 25 *ein Zimmer im Hotel reservieren lassen*
to reserve the right 62 *sich das Recht vorbehalten*
responsibility, to accept ~ 99 *die Verantwortung übernehmen*
résumé 106 *Lebenslauf*
retail outlet 43 *Einzelhandelsgeschäft*
retail price 67 *Einzelhandelspreis*
return if undelivered 13 *Zurück, falls unzustellbar*
reunification 21 *Wiedervereinigung*
to revise 59 *verändern*
revised discounts/prices 30 *neuen Rabatte/Preise*
revised terms 60 *verbesserte Bedingungen/Konditionen*
road, by ~ 50 *per LKW*
rota basis, on a strict ~ 75 *genau der Reihe nach*
rotation, in strict ~ 81 *genau der Reihe nach*
rough 102 *grob, unvorsichtig*
rush of orders 78 *Auftragsflut*

S

safety regulations 46 *Sicherheitsregeln, Sicherheitsvorschriften*
sale, on ~ or return 47 *mit Rückgaberecht, in Kommission*
sales literature 45 *Verkaufsunterlagen*
sales material 47 *Prospektmaterial, Prospekte*
salutation 6 *Grußformel, Anrede*
sample 38 *Muster, Probe(stück)*
satisfactory 25 *zufrieden stellend*
scratched 97 *verkratzt*
to scroll 8 *scrollen*
sea, by ~ 50 *per Seefracht*
sender 4 *Absender/in*
services 48 *Dienstleistungen*
settlement (of invoice) 52 *(Rechnung)Begleichung*
shade 95 *Farbton*
to ship 69 *versenden, verfrachten, verschiffen*
shipment 70 *Sendung, Ladung, Lieferung, Partie*
shipment, ready for ~ 63 *versandfertig, versandbereit*
shipper 81 *Versender, Absender; Spedition(sfirma)*
shipping agent 81 *Spediteur, Seespediteur, Spedition*
shipping instructions 81 *Versandanweisungen*
to sign 6 *unterschreiben*
signature block 6 *Unterschriften*
signed, to be ~ 16 T *ausgeschildert sein*
single room 36 *Einzelzimmer*
to be situated in 25 *gelegen, ansässig sein in*
skills 106 *Fertigkeiten, Kompetenz*
sleeping bag 54 *Schlafsack*
small print, in ~ 48 *klein gedruckt*
solicitor 84 *(Rechts)Anwalt, Anwältin*
space 7 *Leerstelle*
special delivery 13 *durch Eilboten*
special terms 48 *Sonderbedingungen*
specialist 14 *Fach-*
specific 64 *hier: genau*
specifications, to make to customer's ~ 69 *nach Kundenangaben herstellen/anfertigen*
to specify 58 *genaue Angaben machen zu*
specimen 42 *Muster, Probe(stück)*
staff 27 *Mitarbeiter, Personal*
stand (at a trade fair) 41 *(Messe)Stand*

statement, (account) ~ 91 *Kontoaufstellung, Kontoauszug*
statement, quarterly ~ 91 *Quartalsabrechnung, vierteljährliche Abrechnung*
to stipulate 73 *festlegen*
stock, to be in ~ 62 *vorrätig sein*
stock, to be out of ~ 58 *nicht (mehr) vorrätig sein*
stock levels, adequate ~ 68 *ausreichender (Waren)Bestand*
stockist 112 *Fachhändler, Fachgeschäft*
stores 52 *Lager*
student representative council (SRC) 109 *Fachschaft*
subject line 6 *Betreffzeile*
subject to confirmation 51 *freibleibend, unverbindlich*
to submit 50 *vorlegen*
submit a (firm) offer 40 *ein (verbindliches) Angebot machen*
substandard 63 *minderwertig*
substantially 99 *erheblich*
sub-supplier 79 *Unterlieferant*
to suggest a date 30 *ein Datum vorschlagen*
suitable 33 *passend, geeignet*
sum, outstanding ~ 83 *fälliger/offener Betrag*
sum, remaining ~ 89 *Restbetrag*
sunshade 64 *Sonnenschirm*
supplier 5 *Lieferant*
to supply 41 *liefern*
to supply a reference 107 *eine Referenz angeben/mitteilen*
to supply an address 117 *eine Anschrift angeben/mitteilen*
supply contract 79 *Liefervertrag*
surcharge 34 T *Zuschlag*
survey 100 *Untersuchung, Überblick*

T

to tally with 89 *übereinstimmen mit*
to tamper with sth 103 *sich an etw. zu schaffen machen*
tax 32 *Steuer*
temp; temping 117 *Zeitarbeiter/in; Zeitarbeit, Leiharbeit*
temporarily 78 *zeitweilig*
to tend 4 *die Tendenz haben, etw. zu machen*
tender 52 *Angebot (für eine Ausschreibung)*
tent 54 *Zelt*
terms and conditions, (general) ~ 58 *Allgemeine Geschäftsbedingungen*
terms (and conditions) of business 45 *Geschäftsbedingungen*
terms of payment (and delivery) 42 *(Liefer- und) Zahlungsbedingungen*
terms of the offer 58 *Angebotsbedingungen*
testimonial 106 *Referenz, Empfehlungsschreiben*
testing purposes, for ~ 43 *zu Prüfungszwecken*
to be tied up 26 *beschäftigt sein, zu tun haben*
top-quality 68 *hochwertig, von erstklassiger Qualität*
torn 102 *zerrissen*
total 52 *Gesamtsumme*
trade discount 42 *Handelsrabatt*
trainee 117 *Auszubildende/r in einem kaufmännischen Beruf*
traineeship 113 *(kaufmännische) Ausbildung*
to transfer 83 *überweisen*
transit, in ~ 99 *auf dem Transportweg, unterwegs*
transport arrangements 69 *Transportvereinbarungen*
travel arrangements 25 *Reisepläne*
Travel Management Assistant 107 *Reiseverkehrskaufmann/-frau*
travel plans 33 *(Reise)Route*
trial order 57 *Probeauftrag*

to type 9 *tippen, eingeben*
typing mistake 90 *Tippfehler*

U

undersigned 51 *Unterzeichner*
unlimited 34 T *unbegrenzt*
unnoticed, to go ~ 85 *übersehen werden*
unsolicited application 106 *Initiativ-, Blindbewerbung*
upmarket 43 *anspruchsvoll*
urgency 94 *Dringlichkeit*
urgent 33 *dringend*

V

valid 51 *gültig*
venue 16 T *(Veranstaltungs)Ort*
video projector 31 *Beamer*
view, in ~ of 64 *angesichts*
view, with a ~ to 33 *mit der Absicht, zu ...*
vocational training 108 *(Berufs)Ausbildung*
volume discount 42 *Mengenrabatt*
volume order 27 *Großauftrag*

W

warehousing system 60 *Lagersystem*
warranty 63 *Gewährleistung, Garantie*
watertight 46 *wasserdicht*
week, in the ~ commencing ... 36 *in der Woche vom ...*
well-established 47 *gut eingeführt*
wholesale 5 *Großhandel*
wholesaler 41 *Großhändler*
to be willing 43 *bereit sein, etw. zu tun*
to wipe out 89 *zunichte machen*
wishes, with best ~ 10 *Mit den besten Wünschen*
to wonder 33 *überlegen, sich fragen*
work placement, to do a ~ 108 *ein Praktikum machen*
workmanship 64 *Verarbeitung*

Z

ZIP code 7 *Postleitzahl*
zip-fastener 43 *Reißverschluss*

Transcripts

2 Unit 2 Exercise A1

Lisa: Guten Morgen. UB Consult GmbH. Lisa Schmitz. Was kann ich für Sie tun?
Sam: Oh, good morning. Uhm … Look, do you mind if I speak English, please?
Lisa: Not at all. Go ahead.
Sam: Thanks. Can I speak to Ms Bach, please?
Lisa: Of course. Who's calling, please?
Sam: My name's Kavanagh, Sam Kavanagh.
Lisa: Could you spell that for me, please?
Sam: Sure. It's K-A-V-A-N-A-G-H.
Lisa: Sorry, is that G for Golf and H for Hotel?
Sam: Yes, that's right, but we don't pronounce them.
Lisa: Okay, I've got that. Could you hold the line, please, Mr Kavanagh? I'll put you through.
Sam: Thanks a lot. (pause with music)
Lisa: Hello? Mr Kavanagh?
Sam: Yes?
Lisa: I'm so sorry, but Ms Bach's not in her office. She had to go out, I'm afraid. Can I take a message for her?
Sam: Yes. Can you ask her to ring me, please? The number's 00353 for Ireland, then 91 for Galway, then 572231.
Lisa: I've got that. International code 00353, then 91 572231, right?
Sam: That's right. Oh, and could you tell her it's quite urgent, please? I'm away for the rest of the week.
Lisa: Okay. I'll make sure she has your message as soon as she gets back.
Sam: Thanks very much. Goodbye.
Lisa: Bye now, Mr Kavanagh.

3 Unit 2 Exercise A2

Lisa: Guten Tag. UB Consult GmbH. Was kann ich für Sie tun?
Kate: Lisa? It's Kate Connors here.
Lisa: Oh, hello, Kate. How're you?
Kate: Fine, thanks, Lisa. And you?
Lisa: I'm fine, too, thanks. Now, what can I do for you?
Kate: Well, I'm just calling to fix a date and time for Sam's meeting with Mr and Mrs Bach at the Ispo Sportmode fair in Munich next month.
Lisa: Oh, yes. Just a moment, Kate. Mr Bach gave me some dates and times.
(pause).
Kate?
Kate: Yes?
Lisa: Well, how about Saturday, the first at nine-thirty? That's on the first day of the fair.
Kate: Oh, that's just fine, Lisa. Sam's free then. Now, did Mr Bach say anything about the venue?
Lisa: Well, Mr Bach has booked a room for Saturday morning. Could you ask Mr Kavanagh to go to room eight on the first floor of the small conference centre near the Theresienhöhe entrance to the exhibition ground?
Kate: Oh, dear. Where was that, Lisa?
Lisa: Well, the small conference centre is just inside the Theresienhöhe entrance to the exhibition ground. But that shouldn't be a problem. Everything's very well signed in German and English.
Kate: Fine, I've got that, I think, but let me just check – nine-thirty on the first of February in room eight on the first floor of the conference centre at the Theresienhöhe entrance to the exhibition ground, right?
Lisa: That's right, but I'll email to confirm anyhow. Well, thanks for calling, Kate, and please tell Mr Kavanagh that Mr and Mrs Bach are looking very forward to meeting him.
Kate: I'll certainly do that. Well, take care, Lisa. Goodbye.
Lisa: Bye now, Kate.

4 Unit 2 Exercise C7

Jane: Good afternoon. Carr & Sons Limited. Can I help you?
Ben: Good afternoon. Can you put me through to Ms King's office, please?
Jane: Certainly. Who's calling, please?
Ben: My name's Ben Todd.
Jane: Hold the line, please, Mr Todd.

Ann: Good afternoon. Ms King's office. Ann Johnson speaking.
Ben: Good afternoon. It's Ben Todd here. May I speak to Ms King, please?
Ann: I'm sorry. I'm afraid Ms King is in a meeting at the moment.
Ben: Oh, dear. Do you know when she'll be free? I'll call again later.
Ann: Well, I'm afraid I don't know when the meeting will be over. But can I take a message?
Ben: Oh no, thank you. It's private. I'd rather send an email. Thank you. Bye.
Ann: Goodbye.

5   Unit 3 Exercise C6

Kim: Good morning. Star Car Hire. I'm Kim Cameron. Can I help you?
Joe: Hi. My name's Joe Davis. Look, I've a question first. Is it possible to hire a car from Aberdeen Dyce airport but return it at Glasgow Airport?
Kim: No problem, sir. There's a Star office at all Scottish airports.
Joe: Fine. In that case, what would a car cost for five days, please?
Kim: What class of car are you thinking of, sir? We have five groups from a VW Polo or a Ford Fiesta in Group A through to luxury limousines in Group E.
Joe: Well, the car's not for me, actually. It's for my boss. But I know she wants to do a lot of touring, so the car should be comfortable. She doesn't want anything luxurious, though.
Kim: In that case, I'd suggest Group C, sir. What about an Audi A4 or a Peugeot 307, for example?
Joe: The Peugeot sounds good. She drives a Peugeot herself. How much is the 307, then?
Kim: Well, that depends on the day of the week. Weekends are much cheaper.
Joe: Well, she wants to pick the car up at nine am on Monday, the sixteenth of March at Dyce and return it at six pm on Friday, the twentieth at Glasgow Airport.
Kim: Thanks. So that's Group C for four days and nine hours during the week. Just a moment, please. Er ... that's two hundred and eleven pounds ninety-nine.
Joe: Good heavens. That's a lot, isn't it? Does that price include a full tank of petrol?
Kim: No, it doesn't, sir. The tank's full when you pick up the car, of course, but you have to give it back with a full tank as well. If you don't, you have to pay a ten pound surcharge in addition to the cost of our filling the tank, I'm afraid.
Joe: I see. Are there any other extras?
Kim: No. Petrol is the only extra. The price includes full insurance and unlimited mileage.
Joe: Ah, so there's no mileage surcharge?
Kim: No, sir – and that's important if you're touring.
Joe: Okay, then. Look, can I get back to you later? I'm sure it'll be okay, but I'd better check with my boss before making a firm reservation.
Kim: Sure. No problem, sir. We're open at Dyce until 10 pm, by the way.
Joe: Fine. Well, thanks for your help. Bye now.
Kim: You're welcome. Goodbye, sir.

6   Unit 4 Exercise A1

Pia: Guten Morgen. Textil Dorn. Pia Marx am Apparat.
Jane: Oh, ... Is there anyone I can talk to who speaks English, please?
Pia: Of course. How can I help you?
Jane: Well, my name's Jane Adams from Style Four in London. I'd like to speak to somebody in export, please.
Pia: Well, we don't have a separate export department, I'm afraid. I'll put you through to Mr Dorn.

(pause)

Dorn: Dorn.
Jane: Oh, good morning, Mr Dorn. My name's Jane Adams from Style Four in London.
Dorn: Good morning, Ms Adams. What can I do for you?
Jane: Well, we're looking for denim cloth for our new line in jeans. Do you supply that kind of material?
Dorn: Yes, we do. We act as European agents for a number of manufacturers. What are you looking for exactly?
Jane: Well, at the moment we're interested in high-quality light stretch denim in various colours for our summer collection. Can you help us there?
Dorn: Yes, we can. We can offer an excellent range of Italian denim at very competitive prices, for example.
Jane: That sounds interesting. Could you send us samples in various colours?
Dorn: Of course. We can send you our standard collection of samples and then we can take it from there.
Jane: Thank you. I'll fax you the details. (...)

7   Unit 5 Exercise C5

Pat: Good morning. Wessex Fitness Technology. Pat King speaking.
Jo: Hi. It's Top Fit Studios in Southport here. I'm calling about our enquiry for digital ...
Pat: Sorry, can we take it one step at a time, please? Who's speaking, please?
Jo: Oh, sorry. My name's Jo Clarke. That's Jo without an 'e', and Clarke with one.
Pat: Fine. And you're calling from?
Jo: Top Fit Studios, Southport.
Pat: Okay, I've got that. Now, you're ringing about an enquiry, right?
Jo: Right. I'm calling about our enquiry for digital pulse counters.
Pat: Can you give me the details, please? I need the date, reference number, if any, and if possible the catalogue number, okay?
Jo: Sure. The date's the twenty-first of October. The reference number's JC/2110/PC, and the catalogue number is DPC-4X.
Pat: Okay, I've got that. Now, what's the trouble exactly?
Jo: Well, we still haven't received your offer, and things are

getting a bit urgent this end. We already have several orders ourselves.
Pat: Oh, dear. Something's gone wrong here, I'm afraid. Could you hold on a moment, please? (pause) Hello?
Jo: Hello.
Pat: Well, I can't understand it. This offer went out by post on the twenty-fifth of October. You should have got it, well, a week ago.
Jo: Oh, the post again. Great. Could you do me a favour? Could you fax us a copy?
Pat: Of course. What's the number? It'll save me ...
Jo: Sure. 01714 for Southport, then 996603, okay?
Pat: Fine. 01714, then 996603, right?
Jo: That's right. Oh, and I don't want to put you under pressure but could you do that very soon?
Pat: Don't worry. I'll do it immediately.
Jo: Great. Bye now.
Pat: Bye.

8 Unit 6 Exercise C4

Schmieder: Good morning Mr Wilcox. This is Marc Schmieder. I hear you came back from Glasgow yesterday. Did you have a good trip?
Wilcox: Hello Herr Schmieder. Thank you. Yes, I did. I had a very useful talk with Jeremy Scott of Strathclyde Engineering Ltd about your company's offers for machine tools. I'm almost sure he'll order several types of your machines. We also got a number of new orders, too.
Schmieder: I'm pleased to hear that.
Wilcox: Yeah, we are as well. There is one problem though. And that's the value of the euro.
Schmieder: What do you mean?
Wilcox: Well, you see, with the euro going up against the pound, your machines are getting expensive for the British market.
Schmieder: Mmh. I see. And what would you suggest our company should do?
Wilcox: Well, one solution would be to send your invoices in pounds, of course. Otherwise, you could lower your prices a bit or let us have more generous payment terms. That would also help to keep prices down.
Schmieder: Well, to be quite honest, I don't think the management would agree to invoicing in pounds as it would put the entire risk on us. But I'll let my boss know about your suggestion concerning payment terms and get back to you. We certainly don't want to lose the British market now that things are beginning to look up.
Wilcox: I'm glad you understand our problem. And I shall be looking forward to hearing from you. Prices are very important to our customers. I'll also fax the new orders within the next couple of days.
Schmieder: Ok, thanks. So I'll get back to you as soon as I can.
Wilcox: That's fine. Bye for now.
Schmieder: Bye.

9 Unit 7 Exercise C6

Conversation 1

Cunningham: Good morning. This is Mr Cunningham from Atlanta Exports and Imports. Is Ms Kourgialis in?
Secretary: I'm sorry. Ms Kourgialis has gone out to see a customer. She's just rung to say she won't be back in today. Can I take a message?
Cunningham: Yes, thank you. That would be very kind. Would you just tell her that I phoned and ask her to call me back as soon as possible, please?
Secretary: I'm sorry. Could you just give me your name and your company again, please? I'll make sure Ms Kourgialis gets the message as soon as she comes in again tomorrow.
Cunningham: That would be fine. Thank you. So, my name is Cunningham. I'll spell it for you: C-U-N-N-I-N-G-H-A-M. And I'm phoning on behalf of Atlanta Exports and Imports Inc. Ms Kourgialis has got the number.
Secretary: OK, that's fine then. Thank you, Mr. Cunningham. I'll pass on your message as soon as I can.
Cunningham: Good. Thank you very much for your help.

Conversation 2

Kourgialis: Good morning, Mr Cunningham. You tried to reach me yesterday. I'm sorry I wasn't in but I had to go out and see a customer.
Cunningham: Nice of you to call me back so quickly. My boss, Ms Smith, asked me to phone about the order we placed for an important customer of ours. She says they are in urgent need of the parts they ordered.
Kourgialis: I know what you are talking about. I did tell her before that there's been some trouble with this order.
Cunningham: Well, let me see now. Your manufacturers quoted delivery at the beginning of July. That's right isn't it?
Kourgialis: That's right.
Cunningham: But the day before yesterday we were told that the equipment can't be delivered until mid-August at the earliest. In the meantime, however, my principal has opened the letter of credit as agreed.

Kourgialis:	I'm very sorry there's going to be a delay but there's very little I can do. You see, I phoned the manufacturers this morning. And they've promised to dispatch the equipment in the second week of August.
Cunningham:	The point is that work on the construction site could be seriously delayed. Ms Smith suggested you could perhaps get your manufacturer to ship at least part of the consignment in July?
Kourgialis:	Well, you know, two units are in fact ready for dispatch. But the letter of credit says partial deliveries are not allowed.
Cunningham:	We'll talk to the principal, Mr Moss, again. If he agrees that the two units should be dispatched now, we can change the letter of credit accordingly.
Kourgialis:	I'm sorry about that. But I'm afraid, that's all we can do at present.
Cunningham:	Well, I'll phone you again as soon as I know what's happening.
Kourgialis:	OK, you do that. And I'm sorry I can't help any further.

10 Unit 8 Exercise C6

Loewe:	Guten Morgen. Fischer KG. Loewe am Apparat.
Matthews:	Hello, Mr Loewe. Ms Matthews here from Barnes & Hopkins.
Loewe:	Good morning. I hope you enjoyed the nice weather at the weekend.
Matthews:	Yes, thank you. I hope you did, too. Anyway, I have a little problem that I hope you can help me with.
Loewe:	Oh dear. What's the problem?
Matthews:	Well, your last invoice doesn't seem to make sense. It's invoice no. 23678 of 29 March.
Loewe:	OK. Let me find that on my computer... Here we are. Number 23678 of 29 March?
Matthews:	Yes, that's it. Well, you see, the quantities listed in the invoice don't tally with those on your packing list. The quantities you sent us were perfectly correct and matched your packing list. So, that part is OK. But on the invoice they are all different.
Loewe:	Hmm. That shouldn't happen with our computer system because invoices are automatically generated at the same time as the packing lists. I don't understand that.
Matthews:	Some of the prices are also a bit different and we normally get a cash discount but it isn't there.
Loewe:	Really strange. Let's just check the customer number. What does it say on your copy of the invoice?
Matthews:	It says: 453 ... Hey, wait a minute. That's not our number.
Loewe:	Well, there must have been some mix-up with another customer. I'll ask accounts to look into it and get back to you later. Is that OK?
Matthews:	Yeah, that's fine with me. Thank you very much.
Loewe:	You're welcome. Bye now.
Matthews:	Bye.

11 Unit 9 Exercise C5

Helen:	Hello. Is that Katja speaking?
Katja:	Yes, that's right. Hello.
Helen:	Hi, it's Helen Charlton. I've been trying to get hold of you for a while. It can be quite difficult because of the 7 hours time difference between here in Chicago and Germany.
Katja:	Well, you got through in the end. What's the problem, Helen?
Helen:	Well, we seem to be having some problems with your last consignment and your invoice. And I thought we'd better sort that out over the phone.
Katja:	Sorry to hear that. But as you say, it's easier on the phone. Could you just give me the order number and the invoice number so that I can find the details, please?
Helen:	Fine. The order number is 5566/A2
Katja:	That's 5566/A2.
Helen:	That's it. And the invoice number is 293847/05, date: 4 March.
Katja:	So, the invoice number again: 293847/05, date: 4 March ...
Helen:	Right. You see, we have problems with items 2 and 19.
Katja:	Oh, I'm sorry. Let's take one item at a time.
Helen:	Okay. So, item 2. We ordered 50 copies but you only sent us 15.
Katja:	Fine. So we need to send you 35 more then.
Helen:	That's right. Then there is item 19. Here you invoiced more copies than we actually received. You delivered 100 copies but you invoiced us for 150.
Katja:	Well, there's something very badly wrong here. I'm very sorry. These are things that shouldn't really happen. Is that all, Helen?
Helen:	Yes, that's all.
Katja:	Well, I'll certainly ask someone to correct the invoice and cancel the one you've got straightaway. And then I'll send those 35 copies out to you today. But they will take a few days to get to you. Is that OK?
Helen:	That's fine. The main thing is we receive them fairly soon because we've got orders for them.
Katja:	Yeah, sure. I'm really very sorry about this.
Helen:	Don't worry too much. Enjoy the rest of the day.
Katja:	You too. Thank you. Goodbye.

12 Unit 10 Exercise C7

Sheila: Bath 243987

Ms Bryant: This is Liz Bryant from Hunters Ltd in Weston-super-Mare. Is that Mrs. Anderson?

Sheila: No, sorry. This is Sheila Anderson. I'm the daughter actually. Can I take a message?

Ms Bryant: Well ... If your brother is in, I would like to speak to him if I may.

Sheila: Well, my brother Roger is out all day. And I don't know when he'll be back. Can I take a message?

Ms Bryant: Thank you, yes, that would be kind. You see, your brother applied for a job with us.

Sheila: Yes, I know.

Ms Bryant: And I wanted to ask him ... Well, you see he's been short-listed. And I would really like to arrange an interview, if possible.

Sheila: Well, that's good news. He'll be delighted.

Ms Bryant: We'll be interviewing candidates all day next week on Friday. And I had provisionally put his name down for 3 p.m. If that's OK?

Sheila: OK. So, it's Friday at 3 p.m. And where is the interview going to be?

Ms Bryant: We'll be interviewing in the Bristol Crown Hotel to make it easier for candidates. Our office in Weston-super-Mare is difficult to get to. Would you tell your brother, please. And also tell him that if the date and time are not convenient to ring me as soon as possible? If he can make it ask him to report to Reception. They will direct him.

Sheila: Of course, I will. Let me just repeat. So, you want to interview Roger next week on Friday at 3 p.m. And the interview is in the Bristol Crown Hotel. And Roger is to report to Reception. They will direct him. And he is to phone you when he can't make it.

Ms Bryant: That's right. And I'll give you my telephone number. The area code is 01934, and the number is 453 2001. 2001 is my extension. And my name is Liz Bryant.

Sheila: I think I've got that.

Ms Bryant: Good, and thank you. Bye.

Sheila: Bye. And thanks for the good news.

INCO-Terms 2000 im Überblick

Gruppe	Gültig für jede Transportart		Gültig für den Transport zur See oder auf Binnenwasserstraßen	
	Abkürzung	Erklärung	Abkürzung	Erklärung
E	EXW	Ex Works (… named place) *Ab Werk (…benannter Ort)*		
F	FCA	Free Carrier (named place) *Frei Frachtführer (… benannter Ort)*	FAS	Free Alongside Ship (… named Port of Shipment) *Frei Längsseite Schiff (… benannter Ort)*
			FOB	Free On Board (… named Port of Shipment) *Frei an Bord (… benannter Verschiffungshafen)*
C	CPT	Carriage Paid To (… named place of destination) *Frachtfrei (… benannter Bestimmungsort)*	CFR	Cost and Freight (… named Port of Destination) *Kosten und Fracht (… benannter Bestimmungshafen)*
	CIP	Carriage and Insurance Paid To (… named place of destination) *Frachtfrei versichert (… benannter Bestimmungsort)*	CIF	Cost, Insurance and Freight (… named Port of Destination) *Kosten, Versicherung, Fracht (… benannter Bestimmungshafen)*
D	DAF	Delivered At Frontier (… named place) *Geliefert Grenze (… benannter Ort)*	DES	Delivered Ex ship (… named Port of Destination) *Geliefert ab Schiff (… benannter Bestimmungshafen)*
	DDU	Delivered Duty Unpaid (… named place of destination) *Geliefert unverzollt (…benannter Bestimmungsort)*	DEQ	Delivered Ex Quay (… named Port of Destination) *Geliefert ab Kai (… benannter Bestimmungshafen)*
	DDP	Delivered Duty Paid (… named place of destination) *Geliefert verzollt (…benannter Bestimmungsort)*		

Packing containers and materials

Container container

(Holz)Kiste wooden crate

Kasten case

Fass barrel

Ballen bale

Tonne drum

Glas jar

Korbflasche carboy

Beutel bag

Sack sack

Bündel bundle

Palette pallet

Packpapier wrapping paper

Wellpappe corrugated cardboard